READERS RESPOND . . .

Revolution in World Missions was actually a revolution in my mind and heart.

—Marysabel M., Montreal, Canada

I've read *Revolution in World Missions* several times. Just like the message of salvation, the book never grows old.

—Elizabeth K., Queens Village, New York

I started reading it and could not put it down. It was like part two of the book of Acts.

—Gareth W., Staffordshire, England

I just read *Revolution in World Missions*. The Holy Spirit has led me today to stop just going to church but to BE the church!

—Susan S., Altoona, Iowa

Revolution in World Missions made me realize that the difference between poor and rich people is not just a fairy tale, something we see only in movies. This discovery broke my heart.

—Thelma P., Debrecen, Hungary

I was caught up in the book. It made me study and pray more often and harder.

—David S., Jacksonville, Illinois

Revolution in World Missions spoke volumes to me. My budget was/is filled with things that have no eternal value. God convicted my heart!

—Pastor Rudi B., Western Cape, South Africa

I am convinced, having served 20 years as a pastor and in other church ministries, that this is the way missions is supposed to be done!

—Pastor Samuel M., Bluff City, Tennessee

I can tell you that this reading literally blew my mind. It is astonishing to see what God is doing in Asia. I am so excited to be part of this.

—Armando R., Panama City, Panama

I was a Christian who mainly believed that God no longer worked in the same way He did in the book of Acts. When I read *Revolution in World Missions* I realized I was dead wrong.

—James B., Nacogdoches, Texas

I read *Revolution in World Missions*, and I could feel the Lord working in me with every page I read. I felt my heart open to the Lord in a new way and His desires being planted in me.

—Alba S., Toronto, Canada

I was born and raised a missionary kid in Tokyo, Japan, and *Revolution in World Missions* changed my whole perspective.

—Penelope W., Troy, Missouri

I gave *Revolution in World Missions* to my parents to read, and it has generated a lot of interest within our church. Respectfully I request a replacement copy of the book so that I can re-read it.

—Anthony F., Goolwa, South Australia

WHAT INTERNATIONAL CHRISTIAN LEADERS SAY . . .

There are many that talk a good message, but not too many who actually live it out. GFA has what it takes to penetrate the 10/40 Window.

> —DR. LUIS BUSH, International Facilitator
> of Transform World Connections

Gospel for Asia has become one of the more significant pioneer missionary agencies, with a good accountability structure. . . . They are doing an excellent job.

> —PATRICK JOHNSTONE, Author
> Emeritus of *Operation World*

Gospel for Asia is not a movement, but a phenomenon. GFA has become one of the most significant mission organizations of this century.

> —DR. GEORGE VERWER, Founder and former International
> Director of Operation Mobilization

K.P. Yohannan leads one of the largest, if not the largest missionary movement, working across Southeast Asia to bring the love of Christ to the most unreached. . . . The impact of GFA's ministry in Asia is very significant.

> —DR. JOSEPH D'SOUZA, Executive Director
> of Operation Mobilization India

Revolution in World Missions is one of the great classics of Christian literature. It is essential reading for those who desire to obey the mission of Jesus Christ. We get so used to apathetic and halfhearted ideas about missions . . . and then K.P.'s book turns our world upside down!

—Rev. Dr. Paul Blackham, CEO of
Biblical Frameworks, London

You need to read *Revolution in World Missions*. For a guy in our generation to be speaking these words—I don't know that anyone else is saying them as clearly as he is. It's a ministry that I not only endorse, but it's the model of how I want to continue in ministry for the rest of my life.

—Pastor Francis Chan,
Author of *Crazy Love*

My guess is that few realize the extraordinary breadth and depth of the ministry outreach of Gospel for Asia. When I journeyed to South Asia, I was astonished at GFA's amazing outreach and witness for Christ.

—Dr. Frank Wright, President and CEO
of D. James Kennedy Ministries

We are very particular when it comes to partnering with other ministries. But we don't have any hesitation when it comes to Gospel for Asia.

—Ray Comfort, CEO of Living Waters and
Co-Host of *The Way of the Master*

*"To open their eyes, and to turn them from
darkness to light, and from the power of Satan unto God,
that they may receive forgiveness of sins, and inheritance
among them which are sanctified by faith that is in me."*

Acts 26:18

K. P. Yohannan

REVOLUTION
IN WORLD MISSIONS

ONE MAN'S JOURNEY
to CHANGE *a* GENERATION

MORE THAN 3.9 MILLION COPIES IN PRINT

Revised and Updated

gfa
BOOKS

A DIVISION OF GOSPEL FOR ASIA
WWW.GFA.ORG

Revised and Updated Edition © 2017
ISBN: 978-1-59589-169-3
Library of Congress Control Number: 2016940449

Scripture taken from the New King James Version. Copyright © 1982 by Thomas Nelson, Inc. Used by permission. All rights reserved.

Published by gfa books, a division of Gospel for Asia
1116 St. Thomas Way, Wills Point, TX 75169 USA
Phone: (800) 946-2742

Printed in the United States of America

1st printing, July 1986	*20th printing, November 1998*	*39th printing, June 2012*
2nd printing, November 1986	*21st printing, March 2000*	*40th printing, May 2013*
3rd printing, May 1987	*22nd printing, April 2001*	*41st printing, November 2013*
4th printing, December 1987	*23rd printing, November 2001*	*42nd printing, May 2014*
5th printing, July 1989	*24th printing, June 2002*	*43rd printing, October 2014*
6th printing, May 1991	*25th printing, October 2002*	*44th printing, March 2015*
7th printing, January 1992	*26th printing, May 2003*	*45th printing, September 2015*
8th printing, June 1992	*27th printing, October 2003*	*46th printing, January 2017*
9th printing, August 1993	*28th printing, March 2004*	
10th printing, March 1994	*29th printing, July 2004*	
11th printing, June 1994	*30th printing, January 2005*	
12th printing, March 1995	*31st printing, January 2006*	
13th printing, October 1995	*32nd printing, May 2007*	
14th printing, May 1996	*33rd printing, August 2007*	
15th printing, October 1996	*34th printing, November 2008*	
16th printing, March 1997	*35th printing, October 2009*	
17th printing, July 1997	*36th printing, June 2010*	
18th printing, January 1998	*37th printing, December 2010*	
19th printing, August 1998	*38th printing, October 2011*	

For more information about other materials, visit our website www.gfa.org.

This book is dedicated to George Verwer,
founder and former international director of Operation
Mobilization, whom the Lord used to call me into the
ministry and whose life and example have influenced
me more than any other single individual's.

Contents

FOREWORD

We all are skeptical of Christians with big dreams. We don't know why exactly—perhaps we have met too many who pursued visions but whose personal lives were nightmares.

The first time we remember meeting K.P. Yohannan we brought him home for dinner, and our family dragged this slight Indian along with us to a high school gymnasium to sit through an American rite of passage—an all-school spaghetti supper. Across the paper tablecloth, the garlic bread and the centerpieces—shellacked lunch sacks filled with an assortment of dried weeds and pasta (created by members of the Mains family!)—we heard of a dream to win not only India but all of Asia for Christ.

Since that evening in the noisy gymnasium in West Chicago, Illinois, there have been many more shared experiences—phone calls from Dallas; trips to the cities and backwaters of India; pastors' conferences in open thatched-roofed, bamboo-sided pavilions; laughter; travel on Two-Thirds World roads; and times of prayer.

Very simply said, we have come to believe in K.P.

And we believe in his plan for evangelization that, with the profundity of simplicity, bypasses the complexity of technology and challenges Asians to give up their lives to win their fellow countrymen to Christ.

This book, *Revolution in World Missions*, reveals one of God's master plans to reach the world before the end of time. With absolute confidence we know we can endorse the integrity of its author, a man of God, and we are thrilled with the work of Gospel for Asia.

You can read knowing that those evangelists traveling into the unreached villages of Asia have more heart, more fervor, more passion to spread the Gospel of Christ than most of us who are surrounded by the comforts and conveniences of our Western world.

We know because we have seen them and talked with them, and they have put us to shame.

Internationals are the new wave of the missionary effort. K.P. Yohannan's book paints the picture of how that dream is becoming reality.

This is one dreamer of whom we are no longer skeptical. We think you will find reason to believe as well.

—David and Karen Mains

ACKNOWLEDGMENTS

Hundreds of people have had an impact on this volume—from those who have made suggestions, to those who have given encouragement, to those who have influenced my life and ministry. I want to thank all of them—and all of you—and thank the Lord for placing you in my path.

Of those especially close to me during the long writing, editing and review of this manuscript, I would like to thank William T. Bray, David and Karen Mains, Gayle Erwin, Dave Hicks and Martin Bennett for their honest criticism and unwavering support of this entire project. Special thanks also are due Margaret Jordan, Heidi Chupp and Katie McCall, who typed the manuscript. Thanks to my secretary, Teresa Chupp, and her assistants for their hard work on updated editions. And my sincere thanks to Kim Smith for the long hours and careful attention to detail she spent working on revisions and edits for this new edition. And thank you, Cindy Young, for the beautiful cover you created.

And my special thanks to Bob Granholm, former executive director of Frontiers in Canada, for his suggestions for the revision that helped bring balance and clear up misunderstanding.

Most of all, of course, my greatest debt is to my wife, Gisela, for her careful reading and for suggestions that made the critical difference in several passages. Her emotional and spiritual support made the writing of this book possible. Without her standing beside me and encouraging me during these eventful years, this book—and the message it proclaims—would not have been possible.

INTRODUCTION

This is the story of my journey from a small Indian village to the shores of Europe and North America and from colonial missions to a move of God among national missionaries across the globe. It is my own personal story full of the difficulties I had to overcome and God's amazing provision each step along the way. He is so very faithful.

Missions as it is today is not as it has always been. In the 1980s, most evangelical Christians in the West viewed mission history in terms of two great waves. The first wave broke over the New Testament world as the apostles obeyed the Great Commission. The second wave began around the time of William Carey's pioneer work in 18th-century India, and in the 19th and 20th centuries there was a flood of missionaries to the colonies of the great European powers.

Now around the world today, the Holy Spirit is moving over Asian and African nations, raising up thousands of dedicated men and women to take the story of salvation to their own people. Millions are hearing for the first time about the love of God through these national missionaries. They are humble, obscure pioneers of the Gospel taking up the banner of the cross where colonial-era missions left off. This work of the Holy Spirit among these national believers is the third wave of mission history—the indigenous missionary movement.

What does this mean for us? The call of Christ is for *all* of us to "go" or "send"—to bring His love to all peoples on Earth. This move of the Holy Spirit is an incredible opportunity for us to join in this end-time work of God, to link our hearts with what God is doing across the world and send these national believers out among their own people.

And if God is speaking to you to go, you should go! There has never been a time in history when the call to "go" changed. There are no closed doors for God. The book of Acts and the Church of the early centuries are proof of that. The question to ask ourselves is not "How are *we* going to reach them?" but instead, "How will *they* be reached with the Good News?"

There is a cry now for us to run forward and make our lives count. I truly hope that God will use this book to raise up a generation of believers who are united by and overwhelmed with love for the entire world, especially for those who have never once heard the name of Christ. No one should die without hearing about our Lord Jesus and His love.

VIEW POWERFUL VIDEOS ONLINE

RevolutionBook.org

1

Only the Beginning

The silence of the great hall in Kochi was broken only by soft, choking sobs. The Spirit of God was moving over the room with awesome power—convicting of sin and calling men and women into His service. Before the meeting ended, 120 of the 1,200 pastors and Christian leaders present made their way to the altar, responding to the "Great Commission."

They made the choice to leave home, village and family, business or career and go where they would be hated and feared. Meanwhile, another 600 pastors pledged to return to their congregations and pray for more workers who would go to the needy regions.

I stood silently in the holy hush, praying for the earnest pastors crowded around the altar. I was humbled by the presence of God.

As I prayed, my heart ached for these men. How many would be beaten and go hungry or be cold and lonely in the years ahead? How many would sit in jails for their faith? I prayed for the blessing and protection of God on them—and for more sponsors across the seas to stand with them.

They were leaving material comforts, family ties and personal ambitions. Ahead lay a new life among strangers. But I also knew they would witness spiritual victory as many thousands turned to Christ and helped form new congregations in the unreached villages.

With me in the meeting was David Mains, a serious student of revival. He had joined us in Kochi as one of the conference speakers. He later testified how the Lord had taken over the meeting in a most unusual way.

"It would hardly have been different," he wrote later, "had Jesus Himself been bodily among us. The spirit of worship filled the hall. The singing was electrifying. The power of the Holy Spirit came upon the audience. Men actually groaned aloud. I have read of such conviction in early Church history and during the two Great Awakenings, but I had never anticipated experiencing it firsthand."

But the Lord is not simply calling out huge numbers of national workers. God is at work saving people in numbers we never before dreamed possible. People are coming to know the love of Christ all across Asia at an accelerated rate wherever Christ is being proclaimed. In areas such as China, Malaysia, Myanmar and others, it is not uncommon now for the Christian community to grow as much in only one month as it formerly did in a whole year.

Typical of the many indigenous missionary movements that have sprung up overnight is the work of a brother from India—a former military officer who gave up a commission and army career to help start a Gospel team in an unreached area. He now leads more than 400 full-time missionaries.

Like other indigenous mission leaders, he has discipled 10 "Timothys" who are directing the work. Each of them in turn will be able to lead dozens of additional workers who will have their own disciples.

With his wife he set an apostolic pattern for their workers similar to that of the Apostle Paul. On one mission tour that lasted 53 days, he and his family traveled by bullock cart and foot into some of the most needy areas of an eastern state. There, working in the intense heat among people whose lifestyle was extremely primitive, he saw hundreds come to know the Lord. Throughout the journey, demons were cast out and miraculous physical healings took place daily. Thousands heard the Gospel eagerly. In just one month, he formed 15 fellowships and assigned elders to stay behind and build them up in the faith.

Similar miraculous movements are starting almost everywhere in Asia.

National missionary Jesu Das was horrified when he first visited one village and found no believers there. The people were all worshiping hundreds of different deities, and four men controlled them through their witchcraft.

Stories were told of how these witch doctors could kill people's cattle and destroy their crops with black magic. People suddenly became ill and died without explanation. The destruction and bondage the villagers were living in are hard to imagine. Scars, decay and death marked their faces because they were totally controlled by the powers of darkness.

When Jesu Das told them about Christ, it was the first time they ever heard of a God who did not require sacrifices and offerings to appease His anger. As Jesu Das continued to preach in the marketplace, many people came to know the Lord.

But the leaders in the community were outraged. They warned Jesu Das that if he did not leave the village, they would call on evil spirits to kill him, his wife and their children. Jesu Das did not leave. He continued to preach, and villagers continued to be saved.

Finally, after a few weeks, the witch doctors came to Jesu Das and asked him the secret of his power.

"This is the first time our power did not work," they told him. "After doing our black magic, we asked the spirits to go and kill your family. But the spirits came back and told us they could not approach you or your family because you were always surrounded by fire. Then we called more powerful spirits to come after you—but they too returned, saying not only were you surrounded by fire, but angels were also around you all the time."

Jesu Das told them about Christ. The Holy Spirit convicted each of them of their sin of following evil spirits and of the judgment to come. With tears, they repented and received Jesus Christ as Lord. As a result, hundreds of other villagers were set free from sin and bondage.

Through an indigenous organization in Thailand, where more than 200 national missionaries are doing pioneer village evangelism, one group personally shared their faith with 10,463 people in two months. Of these, 171 gave their lives to Christ, and six new churches were formed. More than 1,000 came to Christ in the same reporting period. Remember, this great harvest is happening in a Buddhist nation that never has seen such results.

Reports like these come to us daily from national outreach teams in almost every Asian nation. But I am convinced these are only the first few drops of revival rain. In order to make the necessary impact, we must see hundreds of thousands more workers sent out. We are no longer praying for the proverbial "showers of blessings." Instead I am believing God for virtual thunderstorms of blessings in the days ahead.

How I became a part of this astonishing spiritual renewal in Asia is what this book is all about. And it all began with the prayers of a simple village mother.

2

"O GOD, LET ONE OF MY BOYS PREACH!"

Achyamma's eyes stung with salty tears. But they were not from the cooking fire or the hot spices that wafted up from the pan. She realized time was short. Her six sons were growing beyond her influence. Yet not one showed signs of going into the Gospel ministry.

Except for the youngest—little "Yohannachan" as I was known—every one of her children seemed destined for secular work. My brothers seemed content to live and work around our native village of Niranam in Kerala, South India.

"O God," she prayed in despair, "let just one of my boys preach!" Like Hannah and so many other saintly mothers in the Bible, my mother had dedicated her children to the Lord. That morning, while preparing breakfast, she vowed to fast secretly until God called one of her sons into His service. Every Friday for the next three-and-a-half years, she fasted. Her prayer was always the same.

But nothing happened. Finally, only I, scrawny and little— the baby of the family—was left. There seemed little chance I would preach. Although I had stood up in an evangelistic meeting at age 8, I was shy and timid and kept my faith mostly to myself. I showed no leadership skills and avoided sports and school functions. I was comfortable on the edge of village and family life, a shadowy figure who moved in and out of the scene almost unnoticed.

Then, when I was 16, my mother's prayers were answered. A visiting Gospel team from Operation Mobilization came to our church to present the challenge of faraway North India. My 90-pound frame strained to catch every word as the team spoke and showed slides of the North.

They told of stonings and beatings they received while preaching Christ in the non-Christian villages of North India. Sheltered from contact with the rest of India by the high peaks of the Western Ghats, the lush jungles of Kerala on the Malabar Coast were all I knew of my homeland. And the Malabar Coast had long nourished India's oldest Christian community, begun when the flourishing sea trade with the Persian Gulf made it possible for St. Thomas to introduce Jesus Christ at nearby Cranagore in A.D. 52. Other Jews already were there, having arrived 200 years earlier. The rest of India seemed an ocean away to the Malayalam-speaking people of the southwest coast, and I was no exception.

As the Gospel team explained the desperately poor condition of the subcontinent—tens of thousands of villages without any hope—I felt a strange sorrow for them. That day I vowed to help bring the love of Jesus Christ to those mysterious states to the North. At the challenge to "forsake all and follow Christ," I somewhat rashly took the leap, agreeing to join the student group for a short summer crusade in needy parts of North India.

My decision to go into the ministry largely resulted from my mother's faithful prayers. Although I still had not received what I later understood to be my real call from the Lord, my mother encouraged me to follow my heart in the matter. When I announced my decision, she wordlessly handed over 25 rupees—enough for my train ticket. I set off to apply to the mission's headquarters in Trivandrum.

There I got my first rebuff. Because I was underage, the mission's directors at first refused to let me join the teams going north. But I was permitted to attend the annual training conference to be held in Bangalore, Karnataka. At the conference I first heard missionary statesman George Verwer, who challenged me as never before to commit myself to a life of breathtaking, radical discipleship.

Alone that night in my bed, I argued with both God and my own conscience. By two o'clock in the morning, my pillow wet with sweat and tears, I shook with fear. What if God asked me to preach in the streets? How would I ever be able to stand up in public and speak? What if I were stoned and beaten?

I knew myself only too well. I could hardly bear to look a friend in the eye during a conversation, let alone speak publicly to hostile crowds on behalf of God. As I spoke the words, I realized that I was behaving as Moses did when he was called.

Suddenly, I felt that I was not alone in the room. A great sense of love and of my being loved filled the place. I felt the presence of God and fell on my knees beside the bed.

"Lord God," I gasped in surrender to His presence and will, "I'll give myself to speak for You—but help me to know that You're with me."

In the morning, I awoke to a world and people suddenly different. As I walked outside, the Indian street scenes looked the same as before: Children ran between the legs of people and cows, pigs and chickens wandered about, vendors carried baskets of bright fruit and flowers on their heads. But I loved them all with a supernatural, unconditional love I'd never felt before. It was as if God had removed my eyes and replaced them with His so I could see people as the heavenly Father sees them—lost and needy but with potential to glorify and reflect Him.

I walked to the bus station. My eyes filled with tears of love. I knew that these people were all heading toward eternity without Christ—and I knew God did not want that. Suddenly I had such a burden for these masses that I had to stop and lean against a wall just to keep my balance. This was it; I knew I was feeling the burden of love God feels for the lost and needy. His loving heart was pounding within mine, and I could hardly breathe. The tension was great. I paced back and forth restlessly to keep my knees from knocking in fright.

"Lord!" I cried. "If You want me to do something, say it, and give me courage."

Looking up from my prayer, I saw a huge stone. I knew immediately I had to climb that stone and preach to the crowds in the bus station. Scrambling up, I felt a force like 10,000 volts of electricity shooting through my body.

I began by singing a simple children's chorus. It was all I knew. By the time I finished, a crowd stood at the foot of the rock. I had not prepared myself to speak, but all at once God took over and filled my mouth with words of His love. I preached the Gospel to the poor as Jesus commanded His disciples to do. As the authority and power of God flowed through me, I had superhuman boldness. Words came out I never knew I had—and with a power clearly from above.

Others from the Gospel teams stopped to listen. The question of my age and calling never came up again. That was 1966, and I continued moving with mobile evangelistic teams for the next seven years. We traveled all over North India, never staying very long in any one village. Everywhere we went I preached in the streets while others distributed books and tracts. Occasionally, in smaller villages, we witnessed from house to house.

My urgent, overpowering love for the village people of India and the poor masses grew with the years. People even began to nickname me "Gandhi Man" after the father of modern India, Mahatma Gandhi. Like him, I realized without being told that if the village people of India were ever to be won, it would have to be by brown-skinned nationals who loved them.

As I studied the Gospels, it became clear to me that Jesus understood well the principle of reaching the poor. He avoided the major cities, the rich, the famous and the powerful, concentrating His ministry on the poor laboring class. If we reach the poor, we have touched the masses of Asia.

The battle against hunger and poverty is really a spiritual battle, not a physical or social one as secularists would have us believe. It is through the love of Christ that we will effectively win the war against disease, hunger, injustice and poverty in Asia. To look into the sad eyes of a hungry child or see the wasted life of a drug addict is to witness the evidence of Satan's hold on this world. All bad things, whether in Asia or the West, are his handiwork. He is the ultimate enemy of mankind, and he will do everything within his considerable power to kill and destroy human beings. Fighting this powerful enemy with physical weapons alone is like fighting an armored tank with stones.

I can never forget one of the more dramatic encounters we had with these demonic powers. It was a hot and unusually humid day in 1970. We were preaching in a place called the "desert of kings."

As was our practice before a street meeting, my seven co-workers and I stood in a circle to sing and clap hands to the rhythm of Christian folk songs. A sizeable crowd gathered, and I began to speak in Hindi, the local language. Many heard the Gospel for the first time and eagerly took our Gospels and tracts to read.

One young man came up to me and asked for a book to read. As I talked to him, I sensed in my spirit that he was hungry to know God. When we got ready to climb aboard our Gospel van, he asked to join us.

As the van lurched forward, he cried and wailed. "I am a terrible sinner," he shrieked. "How can I sit among you?" With that he started to jump from the moving van. We held on to him and forced him to the floor to prevent injury.

That night he stayed at our base and the next morning joined us for the prayer meeting. While we were praising and interceding, we heard a sudden scream. The young man was lying on the ground, tongue lolling out of his mouth, his eyes rolled back.

We knew immediately he was demon-possessed. We gathered around him and began taking authority over the forces of hell as they spoke through his mouth.

"We are 74 of us. . . . For the past seven years we have made him walk barefoot all over India. He is ours. . . ." They spoke on, blaspheming and cursing, challenging us and our authority.

But as three of us prayed, the demons could not keep their hold on the young man. They came out when we commanded them to leave in the name of Jesus.

Sundar was delivered and gave his life to Jesus. Later he went to Bible college, and since then the Lord has enabled him to teach and preach to thousands of people about Christ. Several Indian churches have started as a result of his remarkable ministry—all from a man many people would have locked up in an insane asylum.

This kind of miracle kept me going from village to village for those seven years of itinerant preaching. Our lives read like pages from the book of Acts. Most nights we slept between villages in roadside ditches, where we were relatively safe. Our team always created a stir, and at times we even faced stonings and beatings.

The mobile Gospel teams I worked with—and often led—were just like family to me. I began to enjoy the gypsy lifestyle we lived and the total abandonment to the cause of Christ that is demanded of an itinerant evangelist. We were persecuted, hated and despised. Yet we kept going, knowing that we were blazing a trail for the Gospel in districts that had never before experienced an encounter with Christ.

One such village was in Rajasthan. This was the first place I was beaten and stoned for preaching the Gospel. Often when we were there, our literature was destroyed. It seemed that mobs were always on the watch for us, and six times our street meetings were broken up. Our team leaders began to work elsewhere, avoiding this village as much as possible. Three years later, a new team of national missionaries moved into the area under different leadership and preached again at this busy crossroads town.

Almost as soon as they arrived, one man began tearing up literature and grabbed a 19-year-old missionary, Samuel, by the throat. Although beaten severely, Samuel knelt in the street and prayed for the people in that hateful city.

"Lord," he prayed, "I want to come back here and serve You. I'm willing to die here, but I want to come back and serve You in this place."

Many older Christian leaders advised him against his decision, but being determined, Samuel went back and rented a small room. Shipments of literature arrived, and he preached in the face of many difficulties. Today there are hundreds of precious brothers and sisters worshiping the Lord.

This is the kind of commitment and faith it takes to reach the world with the Good News of Jesus Christ.

One time we arrived in a town at daybreak to preach. But word had already gone ahead from the nearby village where we had preached the day before.

As we had morning tea in a roadside stall, the local militant leader approached me politely. In a low voice that betrayed little emotion, he spoke:

"Get in your vehicle and get out of town in five minutes, or we'll burn it and you with it."

I knew he was serious. He was backed by a menacing crowd. Although we did "shake the dust from our feet" that day, today a church meets in that same village. In order to plant the Gospel, we must take risks.

For months at a time I traveled the dusty roads in the heat of the day and shivered through cold nights—suffering just as many are suffering today to bring the Gospel to the lost. In future years I would look back on those seven years of village evangelism as one of the greatest learning experiences of my life. We walked in Jesus' steps, incarnating and representing Him to masses of people who had never before heard the Gospel.

I was living a frenetic, busy life—too busy and thrilled with the work of the Gospel to think much about the future. There was always another campaign just ahead. But I was about to reach a turning point.

3

The Seeds of Future Change

In 1971, I was invited to spend one month in Singapore at a new institute that had been started by John Haggai. It was still in the formative stages then—a place where Asian church leaders would be trained and challenged to witness for Christ. Today, more than 40 years later, the Haggai Institute leadership training program is world-renowned, and Dr. Haggai is still at the helm.

Haggai was full of stories. In them all, Christians were overcomers and giants—men and women who received a vision from God and refused to let go of it. Diligence to your calling was a virtue to be highly prized.

Haggai was the first person who made me believe that nothing is impossible with God. And in Haggai I found a man who refused to accept impossibilities. If the world was not evangelized, why not? If people were hungry, what could we do about it? Haggai refused to accept the world as it was. And I discovered that he was willing to accept personal responsibility to become an agent of change.

Toward the end of my month at the institute, John Haggai challenged me into the most painful introspection I have ever experienced. I know now it implanted a restlessness in me that would last for years, eventually causing me to leave India to search abroad for God's ultimate will in my life.

Haggai's challenge seemed simple at first. He wanted me to go to my room and write down—in one sentence—the single most important thing I was going to do with the rest of my life. He stipulated that it could not be self-centered or worldly in nature. And one more thing—it had to bring glory to God.

I went to my room to write that one sentence. But the paper remained blank for hours and days. Disturbed that I might not be reaching my full potential in Christ, I began at that conference to reevaluate every part of my lifestyle and ministry. I left the conference with the question still ringing in my ears, and for years I would continue to hear the words of John Haggai, "One thing . . . by God's grace you have to do one thing."

I left Singapore newly liberated to think of myself in terms of an individual for the first time. Up until that time—like most Asians—I always had viewed myself as part of a group, either my family or a Gospel team. Although I had no idea what special work God would have for me as an individual, I began thinking of doing my "personal best" for Him. The seeds for future change had been planted, and nothing could stop the approaching storms in my life.

While my greatest passion was still for the villages of the North, I now was traveling all over India. On one of these speaking trips in 1973, I was invited to teach at the spring Operation Mobilization training conference in Madras (now Chennai). That was where I first saw the attractive German girl. As a student in one of my classes, she impressed me with the simplicity of her faith. Soon I found myself thinking that if she were an Indian, she would be the kind of woman I would like to marry someday.

Once, when our eyes met, we held each other's gaze for a brief, extra moment, until I self-consciously broke the spell and quickly fled the room. I was uncomfortable in such male-female encounters. In our culture, single people seldom speak to each other. Even in church and on Gospel teams, the sexes are kept strictly separate.

Certain that I would never again see her, I pushed the thought of the attractive German girl from my mind. But marriage was on my mind. I had made a list of the six qualities I most wanted in a wife and frequently prayed for the right choice to be made for me.

Of course, in India, marriages are arranged by the parents, and I would have to rely on their judgment in selecting the right person for my life partner. I wondered where my parents would find a wife who was willing to share my mobile lifestyle and commitment to the work of the Gospel. But as the conference ended, plans for the summer outreach soon crowded out these thoughts.

That summer, along with a few co-workers, I returned to all the places we had visited during the last few years in the state of Punjab. I had been in and out of the state many times and was eager to see the fruit of our ministry there.

Punjab, the breadbasket of India, is dominated by turbaned Sikhs, a fiercely independent and hardworking people who have always been a caste of warriors. Before the partition of India and Pakistan, the state also had a huge Muslim population. It remains one of the least reached areas of the world.

We had trucked and street-preached our way through hundreds of towns and villages in this state over the previous two years. Although British missionaries had founded many hospitals and schools in the state, very few congregations of believers now existed. The intensely nationalistic Sikhs refused to consider Christianity because they closely associated it with British colonialism.

I traveled with a good-sized team of men. A separate women's team also was assigned to the state, working out of Jullundur. On my way north to link up with the men's team I would lead, I stopped in at the North India headquarters in New Delhi.

To my surprise, there she was again—the German girl. This time she was dressed in a sari, one of the most popular forms of our national dress. I learned she also had been assigned to work in Punjab for the summer with the women's team.

The local director asked me to escort her northward as far as Jullundur, and so we rode in the same van. I learned her name was Gisela, and the more I saw of her the more enchanted I became. She ate the food and drank the water and unconsciously followed all the rules of our culture. The little conversation we had focused on spiritual things and the lost villages of India. I soon realized I had finally found a soul mate who shared my vision and calling.

Romantic love, for most Indians, is something you read about only in storybooks. Daring cinema films, while they frequently deal with the concept, are careful to end the film in a proper Indian manner. So I was faced with the big problem of communicating my forbidden and impossible love. I said nothing to Gisela, of course. But something in her eyes told me we both understood. Could God be bringing us together?

In a few hours we would be separated again, and I reminded myself I had other things to do. Besides, I thought, at the end of the summer she'll be flying to Germany, and I'll probably never see her again. Throughout the summer, surprisingly, our paths did cross again. Each time I felt my love grow stronger. Then I tentatively took a chance at expressing my love with a letter.

Meanwhile, the Punjab survey broke my heart. In village after village, our literature and preaching appeared to have had little lasting impact. The fruit had not remained. Most of the villages we visited appeared just as lost as ever. The people were still locked in disease, poverty and suffering. The Gospel, it seemed to me, hadn't taken root.

In one town, I felt such deep despair that I literally sat down on a curb and sobbed. I wept the bitter tears that only a child can cry.

"Your work is for nothing," taunted a demon in my ear. "Your words are rolling off these people like water off a duck's back!"

Without realizing I was burning out—or what was happening to me spiritually—I fell into listlessness. Like Jonah and Elijah in the Bible, I was too tired to go on. I could see only one thing. The fruit of my work wasn't remaining. More than ever before, I needed time to reassess my ministry.

I corresponded with Gisela. She had, in the meantime, returned to Germany. I decided I would take two years off from the work to study and make some life choices about my ministry and possible marriage.

I began writing letters abroad and became interested in the possibility of attending a Bible school in England. I also had invitations to speak in churches in Germany. In December, I bought an air ticket out of India, planning to be in Europe for Christmas with Gisela's family.

While there I got the first tremors of what soon would become an earthquake-size case of culture shock. As the snow fell, it was obvious to everyone I would have to buy a winter coat and boots—obvious, that is, to everyone except me. One look at the price tags sent me into deep trauma. For the cost of my coat and boots in Germany, I could have lived comfortably for months back in India.

And this concept of living by faith was hard for Gisela's parents to accept. Here was this penniless street preacher from India, without a single dollar of his own, insisting he was going to school but didn't know where—and, by now, asking to marry their daughter.

One by one the miracles occurred, though, and God met every need.

First, a letter arrived from a friend in Dallas, Texas. He had heard about me from a Scottish friend and invited me to come to the United States for two years of study at what was then the Criswell Bible Institute in Dallas. I replied positively and booked myself on a low-cost charter flight to New York with the last money I had.

This flight, it turned out, also was to become a miracle. Not knowing I needed a special student visa, I bought a nonrefundable ticket. If I missed the flight, I would lose both my seat and the ticket.

Praying with my last ounce of faith, I asked God to intervene and somehow get the paperwork for the visa. As I prayed, this friend in Dallas was strangely moved by God to get out of his car, go back to the office, complete my paperwork and personally take it to the post office. In a continuous series of divinely arranged "coincidences," the forms arrived within hours of the deadline.

Before leaving for America, Gisela and I became engaged. I would go on to seminary alone, however. We had no idea when we would see each other again.

4

I Walked in a Daze

As I changed planes for Dallas at JFK International in New York, I was overcome at the sights and sounds around me. Those of us who grow up in Asia hear stories about the affluence and prosperity of the United States, but until you see it with your own eyes, the stories seem like fairy tales.

Westerners are more than just unaware of their affluence—they almost seem to despise it at times. Finding a lounge chair, I stared in amazement at how they treated their beautiful clothes and shoes. The richness of the fabrics and colors was beyond anything I had ever seen. As I would discover again and again, this nation routinely takes its astonishing wealth for granted.

As I would do many times—almost daily—in the weeks ahead, I compared their clothing to that of the national missionary evangelists whom I had left only a few weeks before. Many of them walk barefoot between villages or work in flimsy sandals. Their threadbare cotton garments would not be acceptable as cleaning rags in the United States. Then I discovered most Americans have closets full of clothing they wear only occasionally—and I remembered the years I traveled and worked with only the clothes on my back. And I had lived the normal lifestyle of most village evangelists.

Economist Robert Heilbroner describes the luxuries a typical American family would have to surrender if they lived among the 1 billion hungry people in the Two-Thirds World:

We begin by invading the house of our imaginary American family to strip it of its furniture. Everything goes: beds, chairs, tables, television sets, lamps. We will leave the family with a few old blankets, a kitchen table, a wooden chair. Along with the bureaus go the clothes. Each member of the family may keep in his wardrobe his oldest suit or dress, a shirt or blouse. We will permit a pair of shoes for the head of the family, but none for the wife or children.

We move to the kitchen. The appliances have already been taken out, so we turn to the cupboards. . . . The box of matches may stay, a small bag of flour, some sugar and salt. A few moldy potatoes, already in the garbage can, must be rescued, for they will provide much of tonight's meal. We will leave a handful of onions and a dish of dried beans. All the rest we take away: the meat, the fresh vegetables, the canned goods, the crackers, the candy.

Now we have stripped the house: the bathroom has been dismantled, the running water shut off, the electric wires taken out. Next we take away the house. The family can move to the tool shed. . . . Communications must go next. No more newspapers, magazines, books—not that they are missed, since we must take away our family's literacy as well. Instead, in our shantytown we will allow one radio. . . .

Now government services must go next. No more postmen, no more firemen. There is a school, but it is three miles away and consists of two classrooms. . . . There are, of course, no hospitals or doctors nearby. The nearest clinic is ten miles away and is tended by a midwife. It can be reached by bicycle, provided the family has a bicycle, which is unlikely. . . .

Finally, money. We will allow our family a cash hoard of five dollars. This will prevent our breadwinner from experiencing the tragedy of an Iranian peasant who went blind because he could not raise the $3.94 which he mistakenly thought he needed to receive admission to a hospital where he could have been cured.[1]

This is an accurate description of the lifestyle and world from which I came. From the moment I touched foot on American soil, I walked in an unbelieving daze. How can two so different economies coexist simultaneously on the earth? Everything was so overpowering and confusing to me at first. Not only did I have to learn the simplest procedures—like using the pay telephones and making change—but as a sensitive Christian, I found myself constantly making spiritual evaluations of everything I saw.

In Texas, a land that in many ways epitomizes America, I reeled with shock at the most common things. My hosts eagerly pointed out what they considered their greatest achievements. I nodded with politeness as they showed me their huge churches, high-rise buildings and universities. But these didn't impress me very much. After all, I had seen the Golden Temple in Amritsar, the Taj Mahal, the Palaces of Jhans and the University of Baroda in Gujarat.

What impresses visitors from the Two-Thirds World are the simple things Americans take for granted: fresh water available 24 hours a day, unlimited electrical power, telephones that work and a most remarkable network of paved roads. Compared to Western countries, things in Asia are still in the process of development. At the time, we still had no television in India, but my American hosts seemed to have TV sets in every room—and they operated day and night. This ever-present blast of media disturbed me. For some reason, Americans seemed to have a need to surround themselves with sound all the time. Even in their cars, I noticed the radios were on even when no one was listening.

I was amazed at how important eating was in the Western lifestyle. Even among Christians, food was a major part of fellowship events. This, of course, is not bad in itself. "Love feasts" were an important part of the New Testament church life. But eating can be taken to extremes. One of the ironies of this is the relatively small price those in developed countries pay for food. The average person in the United States or Australia spends less than 10 percent of his disposable income on food and has a surplus of US$30,000-plus for other expenses. By contrast, the average person in Pakistan or Vietnam spends more than 30 percent of his disposable income on food and has less than the equivalent of US$1,000 left over for other needs for the entire year.[2] I had lived with this reality every day, but Westerners have real trouble thinking in these terms.

Often when I spoke at a church, the people would appear moved as I told of the suffering and needs of the national evangelists. They usually took an offering and presented me with a check for what seemed like a great amount of money. Then with their usual hospitality, they invited me to eat with the leaders following the meeting. To my horror, the food frequently cost more than the money they had just given to missions. And I was amazed to learn that European and North American families routinely eat enough meat at one meal to feed an Asian family for a week.

Many national missionaries and their families experience hunger—not because they are fasting voluntarily but because they sometimes have no money to buy food. This occurs especially when they start new work far away from their families and community. The need became real to me through the ministry of Brother Paul, one of the national missionaries we would later sponsor.

Millions of poor, uneducated fisher-folk live along the thousands of islands and endless miles of coastal backwaters in Asia. Their homes usually are small huts made of leaves, and their lifestyles are simple—hard work and little pleasure. These fishermen and their families are some of the most unreached people in the world. But God called Paul and his family to take the Gospel to the unreached fishing villages on the east coast of India.

I remember visiting Paul's family. One of the first things he discovered when he began visiting the villages was that the literacy rate was so low he could not use printed materials effectively. He decided that something visual, such as a slideshow, would work better. (This was before DVDs had been invented.) However, he had no projector or money to purchase one. So he made repeated trips to a hospital where he sold his blood until he had the money he needed.

It was exciting to see the crowds his slide projector attracted. As soon as he began to put up the white sheet that served as a screen, hundreds of adults and children gathered along the beach. Mrs. Paul sang Gospel songs over a loudspeaker powered by a car battery, and their 5-year-old son quoted Bible verses to passersby.

When the sun had set, Brother Paul began his slide presentation. For several hours, people sat in the sand, listening to the Gospel message while the sea murmured in the background. When we finally packed to leave, I had to walk carefully to avoid stepping on the children sleeping on the sand.

But the tragedy behind all this was the secret poverty that Paul and his family faced. There was often not enough money in the house for milk. Ashamed to let the non-Christian neighbors know he was without food, Paul kept the windows and doors in his one-room rented house closed so they could not hear the cries of his four hungry children.

On another occasion, one of his malnourished children fell asleep in school because he was so weak from hunger. Even when the teacher punished his children for lack of attention in class, Paul would not tell his secret suffering and bring shame on the name of Christ.

He told me later, "Only God, our children, and my wife and I know the real story. We have no complaints or even unhappiness. We're joyfully and totally content in our service of the Lord. It is a privilege to be counted worthy to suffer for His sake."

Once we learned his need, we were able to send immediate support to him, thanks to the help of generous Christians. But for too many others, the story does not end as happily.

Is it God's fault that men like Brother Paul are going hungry? I do not think so. God has provided more than enough money to meet Paul's needs and all the needs of the Two-Thirds World. The needed money is in the highly developed nations of the West.

As the days passed into weeks, I began with alarm to understand how misplaced are the spiritual values of most Western believers. Sad to say, it appeared to me that for the most part they had absorbed the same humanistic and materialistic values that dominated the secular culture. I sensed an awesome judgment was coming—and that I had to warn God's people that He was not going to lavish this abundance on them forever. But the message was still not formed in my heart, and it would be many years before I would feel the anointing and courage to speak out against such sin.

5

A Nation Asleep in Bondage

Religion, I discovered, is a multi-billion dollar business in the West. One morning, for example, I picked up a popular Christian magazine containing many interesting articles, stories and reports from all over the world—most written by famous Christian leaders in the West. I noticed that this magazine offered ads for 21 Christian colleges, seminaries and correspondence courses; 5 different English translations of the Bible; 7 conferences and retreats; 5 new Christian films; 19 commentaries and devotional books; 7 Christian health or diet programs; and 5 fund-raising services.

But that was not all. There were ads for all kinds of products and services: counseling, chaplaincy services, writing courses, church steeples, choir robes, wall crosses, baptisteries and water heaters, T-shirts, records, tapes, adoption agencies, tracts, poems, gifts, book clubs and pen pals. Probably none of these things were wrong in themselves, but it bothered me that we should have such spiritual luxury while millions were dying without hearing the Gospel even once.

If the affluence of the West impressed me, the affluence of Western Christians impressed me even more. The United States has thousands of Christian book and gift stores, carrying varieties of products beyond my ability to imagine—and many secular stores also carry religious books. All this while more than 4,000 of the world's 7,000 languages are still without a single portion of the Bible published in their own language![1] In his book *My Billion Bible Dream*, Rochunga Pudaite says, "Eighty-five percent of all Bibles printed today are in English for the nine percent of the world who read English. Eighty percent of the world's people have never owned a Bible while Americans have an average of four in every household."[2]

Besides books, Christian magazines and websites flourish. More than 2,400 Christian radio stations broadcast the Gospel,[3] while many countries don't even have their first Christian radio station. A tiny 0.1 percent of all Christian radio and television programming is directed toward the unevangelized world.[4]

The saddest observation I can make about most of the religious communication activity of the Western world is this: Little, if any, of this media is designed to reach unbelievers. Almost all is entertainment for the saints.

The United States, with its 600,000 congregations or groups, is blessed with 1.5 million full-time Christian workers, the equivalent of one full-time religious leader for every 182 people in the nation.[5] What a difference this is from the rest of the world, where nearly 2 billion people are still waiting to hear about the love of Christ. These needy people have only one full-time Christian worker for every 30,000 people,[6] and there are still 10,000 people groups in the world without a single church among them.[7] These are the masses for whom Christ wept and died.

One of the most impressive blessings in Western nations is religious liberty. Not only do Christians have access to Christian radio and television, unheard of in most nations of Asia, but they are also free to hold meetings, evangelize and print literature.

How different this is from many Asian nations in which government persecution of Christians is common and often legal.

Such was the case for Brother P. This national missionary served time in 14 different prisons between 1960 and 1975. He spent 10 out of those 15 years suffering torture and ridicule for preaching the Gospel to his people.

His ordeal began when he baptized nine new believers and was arrested for doing so. These five men and four women also were arrested, and each was sentenced to a year in prison. He was sentenced to serve six years for influencing them.

The prison where they were sent was literally a dungeon of death. About 25 to 30 people were jammed into one small room with no ventilation or sanitation. The smell was so bad that newcomers often passed out in less than half an hour.

The place where Brother P. and his fellow believers were sent was crawling with lice and cockroaches. Prisoners slept on dirt floors. Rats and mice gnawed on fingers and toes during the night. In the winter there was no heat; in summer no ventilation. For food, the prisoners were allowed one cup of rice each day, but they had to build a fire on the ground to cook it. The room was constantly filled with smoke because there was no chimney. On that inadequate diet, most prisoners became seriously ill, and the stench of vomit was added to the other putrefying odors. Yet miraculously, none of the Christians was sick for even one day during the entire year.

After serving their one-year sentences, the nine new believers were released. Then the authorities decided to break Brother P. They took his Bible away from him, chained him hand and foot, then forced him through a low doorway into a tiny cubicle previously used to store bodies of dead prisoners until relatives came to claim them.

In the damp darkness, the jailer predicted his sanity would not last more than a few days. The room was so small that Brother P. could not stand up or even stretch out on the floor. He could not build a fire to cook, so other prisoners slipped food under the door to keep him alive.

Lice ate away his underwear, but he could not scratch because of the chains, which soon cut his wrists and ankles to the bone. It was winter, and he nearly froze to death several times. He could not tell day from night, but as he closed his eyes, God let him see the pages of the New Testament. Although his Bible had been taken away, he was still able to read it in total darkness. It sustained him as he endured the terrible torture. For three months he was not allowed to speak to another human being.

Brother P. was transferred to many other prisons. In each, he continually shared his faith with both guards and prisoners.

I was beaten and stoned for my faith, so I know what it is to be a persecuted minority in my own country. When I set foot on Western soil, I could sense a spirit of religious liberty. Westerners have never known the fear of persecution. Nothing seems impossible to them.

I had always looked to the Western countries as fortresses of Christianity. With their abundance of both spiritual and material things, affluence beyond most nations on earth, and a totally unfettered Church, I expected to see a bold witness. God's grace obviously has been poured out on these nations in a way no other people have ever experienced.

Instead, I found a Church in spiritual decline. North American believers were still the leading givers to missions, but this appeared due more to historical accident than the deep-set conviction I expected to find. As I spoke in churches and met average Christians, I discovered they had terrible misconceptions

about the missionary mandate of the Church. In church meetings, as I listened to the questions of my hosts and heard their
comments about the Two-Thirds World, my heart would almost
burst with pain. These people, I knew, were capable of so much
more. They were dying spiritually, but I knew God wanted to
give them life again. He wanted His Church to recover its moral
mandate and sense of mission.

By faith, I could see a change coming—the Body of Christ
rediscovering the power of the Gospel and their obligation to
it. But for the time being, all I could do was pray. God had not
given me the words to articulate what I was seeing—or a plat-
form from which to speak. Instead He still had some important
lessons to teach me, and I was to learn them in this alien land far
from my beloved India.

6

WHAT ARE YOU DOING HERE?

The Bible says that "some plant" and "others water." The living God took me halfway around the world to teach me about watering. Before He could trust me with the planting, I had to learn the lesson I had not learned in India—the importance of the local church in God's master plan for the world.

It really started through one of those strange coincidences—a divine appointment that only a sovereign God could engineer. By now I was a busy divinity student in Dallas at the Criswell Bible College, intently soaking up every one of my classes. I was able to dig into God's Word as never before. Now I was doing formal, in-depth study, and the Bible was revealing many of its secrets to me.

After my first term, Gisela and I were married, and she joined me in Dallas at the beginning of the next school term, October 1974. Except for preaching engagements and opportunities to share about Asia on weekends, I was fully absorbed in my studies and establishing our new home.

One weekend, a fellow student invited me to fill the pulpit at a Southern Baptist church he was pastoring in Dallas. Strangely challenged and burdened for this congregation, I preached my heart out. Never once did I mention my vision and burden for

Asia. Instead I expounded Scripture verse by verse. A great love welled up in me for these people.

Although I did not know it, my pastor friend turned in his resignation the same day. The deacons invited me to come back the next week and the next. God gave us a supernatural love for these people, and they loved us back. Late that month the church board invited me to become the pastor, at the age of 23. When Gisela and I accepted the call, I instantly found myself carrying a burden for these people 24 hours a day.

More than once, I shamefacedly remembered how I had despised pastors and their problems. Now that I was patching up relationships, healing wounded spirits and holding a group together, I started to see things in a wholly different light. Some of the problems God's people face are the same worldwide, so I preached against sin and for holy living. Other problems unique to Western culture I was completely unprepared to handle.

Although my weight had increased to 106 pounds, I still nearly collapsed when I attempted to baptize a 250-pound new believer at one of our regular water baptisms. People came to Christ continually, making ours a growing, soul-winning church with a hectic round of meetings that went six nights a week.

The days passed quickly into months. When I wasn't in classes, I was with my people, giving myself to them with the same abandonment that characterized my village preaching. We learned to visit in homes, call on the sick in hospitals, marry and bury. Gisela and I were involved in the lives of our people day and night.

This "staying power" and disciple-making were what my earlier ministry had lacked. I saw why I had failed on the mission fields of Asia. Holding evangelistic crusades and bringing people to Christ are not enough: Someone has to stay behind and nurture the new believers into maturity.

LEFT: **K.P.'s mother** faithfully prayed and fasted every Friday for three-and-a-half years, asking God to call one of her sons to be a missionary. Her prayer was answered when K.P. began to serve the Lord at the age of 16.

BELOW: **K.P. Yohannan** (first row, third from left) with an Operation Mobilization evangelism team (circa 1970).

ABOVE: Hopelessness exudes from the eyes of this young family, trapped by walls of caste and the cruel cycle of poverty. God is calling His Church to be the channel through which His grace and mercy can flow to this family and millions like them.

LEFT: Blamed for the death of her husband, this white-clad widow struggles to survive on the outskirts of society, shunned even by her own family. She desperately needs to hear that she is loved and valued by her Maker.

ABOVE: **Filled to overflowing** with the love of Christ, these national missionaries are passionate to share that love with everyone they meet.

LEFT: In 1974, the Lord brought K.P. and Gisela together to serve Him with one purpose and one goal—to live for Him and to give all they have to reach the world with His love.

BELOW: Their children, Daniel and Sarah, prayed from an early age that the Lord would call them to be missionaries. After finishing high school, they went on to study the Word of God at the theological seminary in India, and now both serve the Lord with their own families.

For the first time I began to understand the goal of all mission work: the "perfecting" of the saints into sanctified, committed disciples of Christ. The local church—a group of believers—is God's ordained place for the discipleship process to take place. God's Plan A for the redemption of the world is the Church, and He has no Plan B.

As I shepherded a local congregation, the Lord revealed to me that the same qualities are needed in national missionary evangelists, the men and women who could reach the peoples of Asia. In my imagination I saw these same discipleship concepts being implemented throughout Asia. Like the early Methodist circuit riders who planted churches on the American frontier, I could see our missionaries adding church planting to their evangelistic efforts.

But even as the concept captured me, I realized it would take a host of God's people to accomplish this task. In the Indian Subcontinent alone, hundreds of thousands of villages have never been reached. And then there are China, Southeast Asia and the islands. We would need tens of thousands of workers to finish the task.

This idea was too big for me to accept, so I pushed it from my mind. After all, I reasoned, God had called me to this local congregation here in Dallas, and He was blessing my ministry. I was getting very comfortable where I was. The church supported us well, and with our first baby on the way, I had begun to accept the Western way of life as my own, complete with a house, automobile, credit cards, insurance policies and bank accounts.

My formal schooling continued as I prepared to settle into building up the church. But my peace about staying in America began slipping away. By the end of 1977, I heard an accusing voice every time I stood in the pulpit: "What are you doing here?

While you preach to an American congregation, millions are dying without ever hearing about the love of Christ. Have you forgotten your people?"

A terrible inner conflict developed. I was unable to recognize the voice. Was it God? Was it my own conscience? Was it demonic? In desperation, I decided to wait upon God for His plan. I had said we would go anywhere, do anything. But we had to hear definitely from God. I could not go on working with that tormenting voice. I announced to the church that I was praying, and I asked them to join with me in seeking the will of God for our future ministry.

"I seem to have no peace," I admitted to them, "about either staying in the United States or returning to India."

I wondered, "What is God really trying to say to me?" As I prayed and fasted, God revealed Himself to me in a vision. It came back several times before I understood the revelation. Many faces would appear before me—the faces of Asian men and their families from many lands. They were holy men and women, with looks of dedication on their faces. Gradually I understood these people to be an image of the indigenous Church that is now being raised up to take the Gospel to every part of Asia.

Then the Lord spoke to me: "They cannot speak what you will speak. They will not go where you will go. You are called to be their servant. You must go where I will send you on their behalf. You are called to be their servant."

As lightning floods the sky in a storm, my whole life passed before me in that instant. I had never spoken English until I was 16, yet now I was ministering in this strange language. I had never worn shoes before I was 17. I was born and raised in a jungle village. Suddenly I realized I had nothing to be proud of; my talents or skills had not brought me to America. My coming here was an act of God's sovereign will. He wanted me to cross cultures, marry a German wife and live in an alien land to give me the experiences I would need to serve in a new move of God.

"I have led you to this point," said God. "Your lifetime call is to be the servant to My servants—men whom I have called out and scattered among the villages of Asia."

Knowing that at last I had found my life's work, I eagerly rushed to share my new vision with my church leaders and executives of missionary societies. To my utter bewilderment, God seemed to have forgotten to tell anyone but me.

My friends thought I was crazy. Mission leaders questioned either my integrity or my qualifications—and sometimes both. Church leaders whom I trusted and respected wrapped fatherly arms around my shoulders and counseled me against undue emotionalism. Suddenly, through a simple announcement, I found myself alone and forced to defend myself. Had I not waited for such a clear calling, I would have collapsed under those early storms of unbelief and doubt. But I remained convinced of my call—certain that God was initiating a new day in world missions. Still, no one seemed to catch my enthusiasm.

Secretly I had prided myself on being a good speaker and salesman, but nothing I could do or say seemed to turn the tide of public opinion. While I was arguing that "new wine needed new wineskins," others could only ask, "Where is the new wine?"

My only comfort was Gisela, who had been with me in India and accepted the vision without question. In moments of discouragement, when even my faith wavered, she refused to allow us to let go of the vision. Rebuffed but certain we had heard God correctly, we planted the first seeds by ourselves.

I wrote to an old friend in India whom I had known and trusted for years, asking him to help me select some needy national workers who were already doing outstanding work. I promised to come and meet them later, and we started planning a survey trip to seek out more qualified workers.

Slowly, a portion of our own personal income and resources was sent as missionary support to India. I became compulsive. Soon I could not buy a hamburger or drink a cola without feeling guilty. Gisela and I conformed our lives literally in the light of eternity and the desperate need to reach and fulfill the call of God. It was a joy to make these little sacrifices for the national brethren. Besides, I knew that it was the only way we could get the mission started.

In those early days, what kept me going was the assurance that there was no other way. Western missions alone could not get the job done. Because my own nation and many others were closed to outsiders, we had to turn to the national believers. Even if Western missionaries somehow were permitted back, the cost of sending them would be in the billions each year. National missionaries could do the same for only a fraction of the cost.

But as logical as it all was in my mind, I had some bitter lessons to learn. Giving birth to a new mission society was going to take much more energy and start-up capital than I could have ever imagined. I had a lot to learn about the West and the way things are done here. But I knew nothing about that yet. I just knew it had to be done.

With youthful zest, Gisela and I went to India to do our first field survey. We returned a month later, penniless but committed to organizing what eventually would become Gospel for Asia.

Soon after our return, I revealed my decision to the congregation. Reluctantly we cut the cords of fellowship and made plans to move to Eufaula, Oklahoma, where another pastor friend had offered me some free space to open offices for the mission.

On the last day at the church, I tearfully preached my farewell sermon. When the last good-bye was said and the last hand was grasped, I locked the door and paused on the steps. I felt the hand of God lifting the mantle from my shoulders. God was releasing me of the burden for this church and the people of this place. As I strolled across the gravel driveway, the mystery of Christian service became real to me.

Pastors—like missionary evangelists—are placed in the harvest fields of this world by God. I would not presume to call the national brethren but simply to be a servant to the ones whom God already had chosen for His service.

Once settled in our new home, I sought counsel from older Christian leaders, listening eagerly to anyone who would give me advice. Everywhere I went, I asked questions. However, much of the advice I got was destructive, and we had to learn most of our lessons by painful trial and error. The only way I escaped several disastrous decisions was my stubborn refusal to compromise the vision God had given. If something fit in with what God had said to me, then I considered it. If not—no matter how attractive it appeared—I refused. The secret of following God's will, I discovered, usually is wrapped up in rejecting the good for God's best.

One piece of advice did stick, however. Every Christian leader should have this engraved in his subconscious: No matter what you do, never take yourself too seriously. Paul Smith, founder of Bible Translations on Tape, was the first executive to say that to me, and it is one of the best single fragments of wisdom I have received from anyone.

God always chooses the foolish things of this world to confound the wise. He shows His might only on the behalf of those who trust in Him. Humility is the place where all Christian service begins.

7

"It Is a Privilege"

We began Gospel for Asia without any kind of plan for regular involvement, but God soon gave us one. On one of my first trips, I went to Wheaton, Illinois, where I called on almost all the evangelical mission leaders. A few encouraged me—but not one offered the money we then needed desperately to keep going another day. The friend I stayed with, however, suggested we start a sponsorship plan through which Christian families and individuals could support the work of national missionaries regularly. It turned out to be just what we needed.

The idea—to lay aside one dollar a day for national missionaries—gave us an instant handle for a program anyone could understand. I asked everyone I met if he or she would help sponsor national missionaries for one dollar a day. Some said yes, and that is how the mission began to get regular donors.

We were just starting out though, and we were faced not infrequently with the need to cover our overhead expenses. Time and time again, just when we were at our lowest point, God miraculously intervened to keep us and the ministry going.

One Sunday, when we were down to our last dollar, I drove our old $125 Nova to a nearby church for worship. I knew no one and sat in the last row. When it came time to take the offering, I quickly made an excuse to God and held on to that last dollar.

"This is my last dollar," I prayed desperately, "and I need to buy gas to get back home." But knowing God loves a cheerful giver, I stopped fighting and sacrificed that last dollar to the Lord.

As I left the church, an old man came up to me. I had never seen him before and never have since. He shook my hand silently, and I could feel a folded piece of paper in his palm. I knew instinctively that it was money. In the car, I opened my hand to find a neatly folded $10 bill.

Another afternoon, I sat grimly sulking on our sofa at home. Gisela was busy in the kitchen, avoiding my eyes. She said nothing, but both of us knew there wasn't any food in the house.

"So," said a coy voice from the enemy, "this is how you and your God provide for the family, eh?" Up until that moment, I don't think I had ever felt such helplessness. Here we were, in the middle of Oklahoma. Even if I had wanted to ask someone for help, I didn't know where to turn. Things had gotten so low I had offered to get a job, but Gisela was the one who refused. She was terrified that I would get into the world of business and not have time to work for the national brethren. For her there was no choice. We had to wait on the Lord. He would provide.

As the demonic voice continued to taunt me, I just sat still under the abuse. I had used up my last bit of faith, declaring a positive confession and praising God. Now I sat numb.

A knock came at the door. Gisela went to answer it. I was in no mood to meet anyone. Someone brought two boxes of groceries to our doorstep. These friends had no way of knowing our need—but we knew the source was God.

During those days, our needs continued to be met on a day-to-day basis. I am convinced now that God knew the many

Pass it On!

K.P. Yohannan

ONE MAN'S JOURNEY
TO CHANGE A GENERATION

REVOLUTION
IN WORLD MISSIONS

FREE BOOK REPLACEMENT
WHEN YOU GIVE
YOURS AWAY.

FREE BOOK REPLACEMENT COUPON

GOSPEL FOR ASIA

Give this copy of *REVOLUTION IN WORLD MISSIONS* to a friend, your pastor, or anyone else who would like to read it. Mail the completed card to us and we'll mail you another copy of the book absolutely free! It's a great way to share the ministry of Gospel for Asia.

Please send me another copy of *Revolution in World Missions:*

Please circle: Mr. Mrs. Miss Rev.

Name _____

Address _____

City _____ State _____ Zip _____

Phone ( ) _____

Email _____

☐ I give Gospel for Asia permission to send me emails (i.e. field stories, urgent prayer requests, etc.).
Privacy Policy: Gospel for Asia will not sell, lease or trade your personal information.

I gave my copy to:

Please circle: Mr. Mrs. Miss Rev.

Name _____

Address _____

City _____ State _____ Zip _____

Phone ( ) _____

Email _____

HB71-PB1C

Your stamp on this card is like an additional donation!—Bro. K.P.

fold before tearing

BUSINESS REPLY MAIL
FIRST-CLASS MAIL · PERMIT NO 1 · WILLS POINT TX

POSTAGE WILL BE PAID BY ADDRESSEE

**GOSPEL FOR ASIA
1116 ST THOMAS WAY
WILLS POINT TX 75169-9911**

Support national missions,
read news from the field,
or download additional
resources online at:

WWW.GFA.ORG

trials ahead and wanted to teach us to have faith and trust in Him alone—even when I could not see Him.

In some way, which I still do not really understand, the trying of our faith works patience and hope into the fabric of our Christian lives. No one, I am convinced, will follow Jesus very long without tribulation. It is His way of demonstrating His presence. Sufferings and trials—like persecution—are a normal part of the Christian walk. We must learn to accept them joyfully if we are to grow through them. Gospel for Asia was having its first wilderness experience, and these days were characterized by periods of the most painful waiting I had ever faced. We were alone in a strange land, utterly at the end of our own strength and desperately dependent on God.

Speaking engagements were hard to come by in the early days, but they were the only way we could grow. Nobody knew my name or the name of Gospel for Asia. I still was having a hard time explaining what we were all about. I knew our mission in my heart, but I hadn't learned to articulate it yet for outsiders. In a few short months, I had used up all the contacts I had.

Setting up a speaking tour took weeks of waiting, writing and calling. By the winter of 1980, I was ready to start my first major tour. I bought a budget air ticket that gave me unlimited travel for 21 days—and somehow I managed to make appointments in 18 cities. My itinerary would take me through the Southwest, from Dallas to Los Angeles.

On the day of my departure, a terrible winter storm hit the region. All the buses—including the one I planned to take from Oklahoma to Dallas—were cancelled.

Our old Nova had some engine problems, so a neighbor offered to let me use an old pickup truck without a heater. The vehicle looked as if it could not make it to the next town, let alone the six-hour drive to Dallas. But it was either the pickup or nothing. If I missed my flight, the tightly packed schedule would be ruined. I had to go now.

Doing the best I could to stay warm, I put on two pairs of socks and all the clothing I could. But even with the extra protection, I was on U.S. Highway 75 only a few minutes when it appeared I had made a terrible mistake. A freezing snow covered the windshield within minutes. After every mile I had to stop, get out and scrape the windows again. Soon my feet and gloves were soaked and frozen. I realized that the journey was going to take a lot longer than the six hours I had left. In my worst scenario, I saw the newspaper headlines reading "Preacher Freezes to Death in Winter Storm." My head dropped to the steering wheel, and I cried out to God.

"Lord, if You want me to go—if You believe in this mission and in my helping the national evangelists—please do something."

As I looked up, I saw a miracle on the windshield. The ice was melting rapidly before my eyes. Warmth flooded the truck. I looked at the heater, but nothing was coming out. Outside, the storm continued to rage. It kept up all the way to Dallas, but the truck was always warm, and the windshield was always clear.

This miraculous start was only the beginning of blessings. For the next 18 days, I gained new sponsors and donors in every city. The Lord gave me favor in the eyes of all I met.

On the last day of the tour, a man in California came to the pastor and said that God had told him to donate his second car to me. I cancelled my airline reservation and drove all the way home, rejoicing in the car God had provided. I received new inspiration and instruction from God as I drove.

I followed this pattern for the next few years, surviving from one meeting to the next, living out of the trunk of the car and speaking anywhere I could get an invitation. All our new donors and sponsors came from one-on-one contacts and through the meetings. I knew there were faster, more efficient ways to acquire new donors. Many times I studied the mass mailings and radio/TV broadcasts of other missions, but everything they were doing required large sums of money, which I did not have and did not know how to get.

Eventually, we moved back to Dallas. By now I was traveling full-time for the ministry, and the strain was taking a heavy toll both on my family and on me. I was starting to burn out; I almost hated the work.

Two factors were wearing me down.

First, I felt like a beggar. It is hard on the flesh to be traveling and asking for money day after day and night after night. It was almost becoming a sales operation for me, and I stopped feeling good about myself.

Second, I was discouraged by the poor response—especially from churches and pastors. Many days I called on people for hours to get only one or two new sponsors. Pastors and mission committees listened to me and promised to call back, but I never heard from them again. It always seemed as though I was competing against the building fund, new carpets for the fellowship hall or next Saturday night's Jesus rock concert.

Despite the solemn message of death, suffering and need I was presenting, people still left the meetings with laughter and gossip on their lips. I was offended at the spirit of jocularity in the churches; it wounded me. So many times they went out to eat after I had just shared the tragedy of the thousands starving to death daily or the millions of homeless people living on the streets of Asia. Because of this, I was becoming angry and judgmental. As I felt uglier and uglier inside, depression settled in.

Early in 1981—while driving alone between meetings in a rented car near Greensboro, North Carolina—all the dark feelings of psychological burnout crept over me. I had a full-fledged pity party, feeling sorry for myself and the hard life I was leading.

Then with a start, I began to tremble with fear. Suddenly I felt the presence of someone else. I realized that the Spirit of the Lord was speaking.

"I am not in any trouble," He chided, "that I need someone to beg for Me or help Me out. I made no promises that I will not keep. It is not the largeness of the work that matters, but only doing what I command. All I ask of you is that you be a servant. For all who join with you in the work, it will be a privilege—a light burden for them."

The words echoed in my mind. This is His work, I told myself. Why am I making it mine? The burden is light. Why am I making it heavy? The work is a privilege. Why am I making it a chore?

I instantly repented of my sinful attitudes. God was sharing His work with me, and He was speaking of others who would join me. Although I still was doing the work alone, it was exciting to think others would be joining with me and that they too would find the burden to be light. From that moment until now, I have not been overpowered by the burden of heading Gospel for Asia. I find building this mission an exciting, joyful job. Even my preaching has changed. My posture is different. Today the pressure is gone. No longer do I feel I have to beg audiences or make them feel guilty.

Because the work of Gospel for Asia—and the whole indigenous missionary movement—is initiated by God, it does not need the worries and guidance of man. Whether our goal is to support 10 thousand or 10 million workers, whether it is working in 10 states or 100, or whether I must supervise a staff of 5 or 500, I still can approach this work without stress. For this is His work, and our burden is easy.

By now we had rented offices in Dallas, and the mission was growing steadily. I sensed it was time for a big step forward and waited upon God for a miracle breakthrough. By mid-1981 we had hundreds of national workers needing support, and I realized that we soon would have thousands more. I no longer could communicate personally with every new sponsor. I knew we had to use mass media. But I didn't know where to begin.

Then I met Brother Lester Roloff.

Brother Roloff is now with the Lord, but during his life he was a rugged individualist who preached his way across five decades of outstanding Christian service. Near the end of his life, I approached him for help in our ministry. His staff person, in arranging the interview, said I would have only five minutes. To his staff's astonishment, he gave me two hours of his time.

When I told Brother Roloff about the indigenous missionary movement, he invited me to be his guest on *Family Altar*—his daily radio broadcast. At that time we were helping only 100 national missionaries, and Brother Roloff announced over the air that he personally was going to help support six more. He called me one of the "greatest missionaries he had ever met" and urged his listeners to support the work of national missionaries as well. Soon we were getting letters from all over the country.

As I read the postmarks and the letters, I realized again just how huge the United States and Canada really are. Brother Roloff was the first Christian leader I had met who had done what I knew we needed to do. He had learned how to speak to the whole nation. For weeks I prayed for him, asking God to show me how I could work with him and learn from his example.

When the answer came, it was quite different from anything I had expected. The Lord gave me an idea that I now realize was unusual, almost bizarre. I would ask Brother Roloff to loan me his mailing list and let me ask his people to support national missionaries.

Trembling, I called his office and asked for another appointment. He saw me again but was very surprised at my request, telling me that he had never loaned his list to anyone—even his best friends. Many agencies had asked to rent his list, but he had always said no. I thought my cause was lost, but he said he would pray about it.

The next day he called me back, saying that the Lord had told him to give us his list. He also offered to write a letter of endorsement and interview me again on the radio broadcast at the same time the letter went out. Elated, I praised God. But I soon learned that this was only the beginning of the miracle.

The list was a fairly large one, and printing a brochure, my letter and his letter, together with the mailing, would cost more money than we had. There seemed to be only one way to get it. I would have to borrow—just this once—from the missionary funds that were earmarked to be sent to the field. I figured it out again and again. If I worked it just right, I could get the money to the field with only a few weeks' delay. But I had no peace about the plan.

When the time came to send the regular monies to the field, I told our bookkeeper to hold the money for one day, and I prayed. Still no peace. The next day I told her to hold the money for another day, and I went back to prayer and fasting. Still no peace. I delayed it for a third day—and still God would not release me to use these field funds.

I was miserable. Finally I decided I could not break the trust of our donors—even for the Lord's work. I told my secretary to go ahead and send the missionary money.

I now realize we had gone through one of the greatest tests of the ministry at that time. This was my first chance to get a major increase in donors and income—but it had to be done with integrity or not at all.

A half hour after the check had gone to the field, the telephone rang. It was from a couple whom I had met only once before at our annual banquet in Dallas. They had been praying about helping us, and God had laid me on their hearts. They asked if they could come and talk to me, and they wanted to know what I needed.

After I explained the cost involved for printing and putting out the mailing, they agreed to pick up the entire amount—nearly $20,000. Then the printer became so moved by the project that he did it for free! Plainly God had been testing me, and He miraculously showed that if we were obedient, He indeed would provide.

The artwork went to the printers and soon printed letters were sitting on skids, ready for the post office. I had prepared a special radio broadcast to coincide with the arrival of the mailing—and the broadcast tapes had already been shipped to stations in many parts of the nation.

Timing was everything. The mail had to go on Monday. It was Friday, and I had no money in the general fund for the postage. This time there was no question of borrowing the missionary money. It stayed right where it was.

I called a special prayer meeting, and we met that night in the living room of our home. Finally the Lord gave me peace. Our prayers of faith would be answered, I announced. After everyone had gone home, the telephone rang. It was one of our sponsors in Chicago. God had been speaking to her all day about giving a $5,000 gift.

"Praise God," I said.

That mailing incident proved to be another turning point in the history of Gospel for Asia. We received many new sponsors—a double increase in the number of evangelists we were able to help.

In later years, other Christian leaders, like Bob Walker of Christian Life Missions and David Mains of Chapel of the Air, would help us in similar ways. Many of the people who joined our ministry through those several early mailings have since helped expand the ministry even further, giving us a base of contacts around the world.

8

A NEW DAY IN MISSIONS

Several hundred people now were supporting the work of national workers on the field. But despite this aura of success, many things broke my heart, especially the condition of the Church in the West. What had happened to the zeal for missions and outreach that made these people so great? Night after night I stood before audiences, trying my best to communicate the global realities of our planet. But somehow I was not getting through. I could see their unfulfilled destiny so clearly. Why couldn't they?

Here were people of great privilege—a Church more able, more affluent and more free to act on the Great Commission than in all of history. Yet my audiences did not seem to comprehend this. Even more confusing to me was the fact that in personal dealings I found my hosts to be basically fair, often generous and spiritually gifted. Like the church in first-century Corinth, they appeared to excel in every spiritual blessing.

Why then, I asked the Lord, was I failing to get through? If the indigenous missionary movement was really the will of God—and I knew it was—then why were the people so slow to respond?

Something obviously had gone wrong. Satan had sprung a trap, or perhaps many traps, on the minds of Christians. Plainly they had lost the Gospel mandate, abdicating the heritage of missionary outreach, the call of God that still rests on them.

I was certain then, and still am today, that God's loving hands of grace and forgiveness remain extended to His people. In my prayers I began to seek a message from God that would bring a change in lifestyle to the Western Church. It came over a period of weeks. And that message came loud and clear: Unless there is repentance among Christians—individually and in concert as a community of believers—an awesome judgment will fall on us.

Two reasons, it appeared to me, were the cause for the current malaise that had fastened like cancer on believers. The first is historical. The second is unconfessed sin related to three basic iniquities: pride, unbelief and worldliness.

Historically, the Western Church lost its grip on the challenge for world missions at the end of World War II. Ever since that time, the moral mandate and vision of the Western Church for global outreach have continued to fade. In fact, the average believer today can hardly pronounce the word *missionary* without having cartoon caricatures of ridiculous little men in pith helmets pop into mind—images of cannibals with spears and huge black pots of boiling water.

Despite a valiant rear guard action by many outstanding evangelical leaders and missions, it has been impossible for the Western missionary movement to keep up with exploding populations and the new political realities of nationalism in the Two-Thirds World. Most Christians in the West still conceive of missions in terms of blond-haired, blue-eyed white people going to the dark-skinned Two-Thirds World nations. In reality, all of that changed when the Western powers lost political and military control of their former colonies.

When I stand before audiences in churches and mission conferences, people are astonished to hear the real facts of missions today. The frontline work of missions in Asia has been taken over almost completely by indigenous missionaries. And the results are outstanding. People are shocked to learn that national workers are starting hundreds of new churches every week in the Two-Thirds World, that thousands of people a day are coming to Christ, and that tens of thousands of well-qualified, spiritually able men and women are ready to start more work if they can find the resources to do the job.

In nations that no longer permit Western missionaries, more church growth and outreach are happening now than at any point in history. China is a good example of the new realities. When the communists drove Western missionaries out and closed the churches in 1950, it seemed that Christianity was dead. In fact, most of the known leaders were imprisoned, and a whole generation of Chinese pastors was killed or disappeared in communist prisons and torture chambers.

But today with communication open again with China, we are finding out that nearly 1 million underground churches have sprung up during the communist persecution. Estimates of the number of Christians today in China vary widely, but responsible authorities place it around 100 million, compared to 1 million when Western missionaries were driven out.[1] Again, all this has happened under the spiritual direction of the indigenous Church movement.

Looking back, it is not difficult to trace how Western thinking has been confused by the march of history. In the early 1950s, the destruction of the colonial missionary establishment was big news. For nearly 200 years of colonial rule in Asia, the Great Commission had been accomplished mainly by a handful of foreigners. After World War II, however, when the colonial-era missionaries returned to take back control of the churches, hospitals and schools, they found the political climate had changed. They met a new hostility from Asian governments. Something radical had happened during World War II. The nationalists had organized and were on the march.

Soon political revolution was sweeping the Two-Thirds World. With the independence of one nation after another, missionaries lost the positions of power and privilege they had held under colonial rule. In the 25 years following World War II, 71 nations broke free of Western domination. And with their new freedom, most decided Western missionaries would be among the first symbols of the West to go.

As the doors of China, India, Myanmar, North Korea, North Vietnam and many other newly independent nations slammed shut on Western missionaries, it was natural for the traditional churches and denominational missions to assume that their day had ended. That, of course, was in itself untrue, as evidenced by the growth of evangelical missions in the same period. But many became convinced then that the age of missions had ended forever. Most believers today have lost hope of seeing the Great Commission of Christ fulfilled on a global scale. Indeed, except during the annual missions appeal at their church, few give it a thought. Although it was rarely stated, the implication was this: If Western-based mission boards were not leading the way, then it could not happen.

Mission monies once used to proclaim the Gospel were more and more sidetracked into the charitable social programs toward which the new governments of the former colonies were more sympathetic. Many of the foreign missionaries who did stay on in Asia were also deeply affected, and they began a steady retreat from evangelism and discipleship, concentrating for the most part on relief and social work instead. A convenient theology of missions developed that equates social and political action with the Great Commission of Christ.

True, in many cases it no longer is possible, for political reasons, for Western missionaries to go overseas, but Christians still have a vital role in the Two-Thirds World. I praise God for the pioneer work done in Asia by Hudson Taylor and others like him who were sent to these nations. Now, however, we need to give financial and technical support to national workers who are finishing the task.

Imagine the implications of being involved in the work of the Great Commission, of getting your church and family to join with you in supporting indigenous missions.

Picture this very possible scene. You finish your life on this earth. You arrive in heaven. There, enthroned in all His glory, is our Lord Jesus Christ. The other saints and martyrs you have read about are there: Abraham, Moses, Peter and Paul, plus great leaders from more recent times. Your family and loved ones who obeyed the Gospel are also there. They are all welcoming you into heaven. You walk around in bliss, filled with joy and praises. All the promises of the Bible are true. The streets really are gold, and the glory of God shines brightly, replacing the sun, moon and stars. It is beyond the power of any man to describe.

Then, scores of strangers whom you don't recognize start to gather around with happy smiles and outstretched hands. They embrace you with affection and gratitude.

"Thank you . . . thank you . . . thank you," they repeat in a chorus. With great surprise you ask, "What did I do? I have never seen you before."

They tell you the story of how they came to be in heaven, all because your love and concern reached out to them while they were on earth. You see that these persons come from "every tongue and tribe," just as the Bible says—from India, Bangladesh, Bhutan, Sri Lanka and Malaysia.

"But what exactly did I do?" you ask. Then, like a replay of a movie, your mind goes back to a day in your life on earth when a local mission coordinator came to your church. He told you about the lost millions of Asia. Then he told you about the dedicated, poor national missionaries and challenged you to support their work.

"As a result of your support," the crowd of Asians continues, "one of our own—a national evangelist—came to us and preached the Gospel of the kingdom. He lived simply, just like us, speaking our language and dressed in our clothing. We were able to accept his message easily. We learned for the first time about the love of Jesus, who died on the cross for us, and how His blood redeemed us from sin, Satan and death."

As the crowd finishes, other whole families come up to you. You can see the tenderness and gratefulness on their faces as well. They join the others, taking you in their arms and thanking you again.

"How can we ever express our appreciation for the love and kindness you showed by supporting us on the earth in our service to the Lord? We endured persecution and hardships as we sought to witness to our own people who had never heard the Gospel. Now they are here in eternity with us.

"In the middle of our suffering, you came into our lives with your prayers and financial support. Your help relieved us so much—making it possible for us to carry on the work of the Lord.

"We never had a chance to see you face-to-face in the world. Now we can see you here and spend all eternity rejoicing with you over the victories of the Lord."

Now Jesus Himself appears. You bow as He quotes the familiar Scripture verses to you: "I was hungry and you gave Me food; I was thirsty and you gave Me drink; I was a stranger and you took Me in; I was naked and you clothed Me. . . . Assuredly, I say to you, inasmuch as you did it to one of the least of these My brethren, you did it to Me" (Matthew 25:35–36, 40).

Is this just a fanciful story, or will it be reality for many thousands of Christians? I believe it could happen as Christians arrive in heaven and see how they have laid up treasure where moth and rust cannot corrupt.

Sadly, so many Christians today still have no idea that a new day in missions has dawned and that their support of missions is more desperately needed than ever before. They have yet to realize the place of privilege the Lord has given them and what that can mean for world missions.

9

IS MISSIONS AN OPTION?

If the Apostle Paul had not brought the Gospel to Europe, foundational principles such as freedom and human dignity would not be part of the Western heritage. Because the Holy Spirit instructed him to turn away from Asia and go west, Western nations have been blessed with their systems of law and economics—the principles that made them rich and free.

Think a moment about the vast difference between your country and the poorer nations of the world.

- While many of us struggle with our weight, the poor in this world struggle to find their next meal. In most countries where Gospel for Asia is supporting the indigenous missionary movement, the gross national income per person was approximately US$1,500 a year as of 2014. By contrast, in some of the most economically developed regions of the world it was more than US$50,000 a year.[1] And Christians in these countries, because they tend to live in the upper half of the economy, earn even more!

- In addition to freedom from want, people in most of these free nations enjoy freedom of speech, press and assembly; freedom of religion; freedom to choose where and how to live; and freedom to organize themselves to correct injustices and problems both at home and abroad.

- Large numbers of service networks in communications, education, finance, mass media and transportation add to the quality of life in the West. Not having these services available is an enormous handicap to people living in nations with less fortunate circumstances.

- Finally, few domestic needs exist. Although unemployment is a serious problem in some areas, it is many times higher in nearly every country of the Two-Thirds World. How many of us can comprehend the suffering of the millions of homeless and starving people in nations like Bangladesh? Overseas the problems are on a grand scale. Some nations struggle to help themselves but still fail woefully.

This is just a short list of the many advantages of living in the more affluent world where benefits have come largely because of a Biblical faith.

Every time I stand before an audience, I try early in my message to ask two very important questions that every Christian needs to ask himself:

- Why do you think God has allowed you to be born with such privileges, rather than among the desperately poor slums in our world?

- In light of the blessings you enjoy, what do you think is your minimal responsibility to the untold millions of lost and suffering people in our generation?

Those who have been born into affluence, freedom and divine blessings should be the most thankful people on earth. But along with the privilege comes a responsibility. The Christian must ask not only why, but also what he should do with these unearned favors.

Throughout Scripture, we see only one correct response to abundance: sharing.

God gives some people more than they need so that they can be channels of blessing to others. God desires equity between His people on a worldwide basis. That is why the early Church had no poverty.

The Apostle Paul wrote to the rich Christians in Corinth, "For I do not mean that others should be eased and you burdened; but by an equality, that now at this time your abundance may supply their lack, that their abundance also may supply your lack—that there may be equality" (2 Corinthians 8:13–14).

The Bible advocates and demands that we show love for the needy brethren. Right now, because of historical and economic factors that none of us can control, most of the needy brethren are in Two-Thirds World countries. The conclusion is obvious: We affluent believers must share with them.

"We know that we have passed from death to life, because we love the brethren. . . . But whoever has this world's goods, and sees his brother in need, and shuts up his heart from him, how does the love of God abide in him? My little children, let us not love in word or in tongue, but in deed and in truth" (1 John 3:14, 17–18).

And, "What does it profit, my brethren, if someone says he has faith but does not have works? Can faith save him? If a brother or sister is naked and destitute of daily food, and one of you says to them, 'Depart in peace, be warmed and filled,' but you do not give them the things which are needed for the body, what does it profit? Thus also faith by itself, if it does not have works, is dead" (James 2:14–17).

God has not given us a superabundance of blessings so we can sit back and enjoy luxuries—or even in spiritual terms, so we can gorge ourselves on books and deeper-life conferences. He has left us on this earth to be stewards of these spiritual and material blessings, learning how to share with others and administer our wealth to accomplish the purposes of God.

How are we doing in this regard? The sad facts speak for themselves.

The average Christian gives only pennies a week to global missions.[2] Imagine what that means. Missions is the primary task of the Church, our Lord's final command to us before His ascension. Jesus died on the cross to start a missionary movement. He came to show God's love, and we are left here to continue that mission. Yet this most important task of the Church is receiving far less than one percent of all our finances.

Remember, a high percentage of the missionaries who are sent overseas are not involved in the primary tasks of preaching the Gospel and planting churches. And approximately 85 percent of all missionary finances go to support missionaries who are working among already-established churches on the field— not for pioneer evangelism to the lost.[3] Consequently, most of those pennies given to missions actually are spent on projects or programs other than proclaiming the Gospel of Christ to those who have never heard.

What is the bottom line? God is calling us as Christians to alter our lifestyles, to give up the nonessentials of our lives so we can better invest our wealth in the kingdom of God.

To start, I challenge believers to lay aside at least $1 a day to help support the work of national missionaries in needy nations.

This, of course, should be over and above our present commitments to the local church and other ministries. My challenge is for us to expand our giving over and above current levels.

Most believers can accomplish this easily by simply cutting down on sweets, coffee and junk foods that harm our bodies anyway. Anyone can save enough in this way to help one or even two missionaries. Many are going beyond this and, without affecting health or happiness, are able to help the ministry of several missionaries.

There are, of course, many other ways to get involved. Some cannot give more financially, but they can invest time in intercessory prayer and help recruit more people to give. And a few are called to go overseas to become more directly involved.

Is missions an option—especially for wealthy countries? The biblical answer is clear. Every Christian has some minimal responsibility to get involved in helping the poor brethren in the Church in other countries.

10

GOD IS WITHHOLDING JUDGMENT

As I traveled and addressed God's people, it became apparent that one of the most significant hindrances to reaching our generation for Christ is the lack of total involvement by the Body of Christ. I am convinced that we have the potential to finish the work God gave us to do. However, many Christians still do not even consider what their part is in the Great Commission. How can this be since this is the work Christ left for us to do? Three major reasons why the Body of Christ is falling so far short of the Great Commission are the sins of pride, unbelief and worldliness.

Pride

Ask the average Christian why the Lord destroyed Sodom, and he or she will cite the city's gross immorality. The prophet Ezekiel, however, reveals the real reason in chapter 16, verses 49 and 50: "Look, this was the iniquity of your sister Sodom: She and her daughter had pride, fullness of food, and abundance of idleness; neither did she strengthen the hand of the poor and needy. And they were haughty and committed abomination before Me; therefore I took them away as I saw fit."

Sodom refused to aid the needy poor because of pride. We are caught up in a pride similar to Sodom's. Yes, selfishness and perversion come from that pride, but we need to see that pride is the real root. Deal with that root and you cut off a multitude of sins before they have a chance to grow.

One night while speaking at a church missionary conference, I was asked to meet privately with the church council to give my reaction to a new mission program they were considering. I had already preached and was very tired. I did not feel like sitting in a board meeting. The meeting, attended by 22 persons, began in the usual way, more like a corporate board meeting at IBM or General Motors than a church board.

The Lord spoke to me clearly: "Son, tonight you must speak to people who are so self-sufficient they've never asked Me about this plan. They think I'm helpless."

When the chairman of the church council finally called on me to respond with my opinion of the proposal, I stood and read certain parts of Matthew 28:18–20: "And Jesus came and spoke to them, saying, 'All authority has been given to Me in heaven and on earth. Go therefore and make disciples of all the nations, baptizing them in the name of the Father and of the Son and of the Holy Spirit, teaching them to observe all things that I have commanded you; and lo, I am with you always.'"

Then I closed my Bible and paused, looking each one in the eyes.

"How often have you met for prayer?" I asked rhetorically. "How long since you have had an entire day of prayer to seek God's mind about your mission strategy?" From their eyes it was easy to see they had prayed little about their mission budget, which was then in the hundreds of thousands of dollars.

The discussion went on until 1:30 in the morning, but with a new sense of repentance in the room.

"Brother K.P.," said the leader to me afterward, "you have destroyed everything we were trying to do tonight, but now we're ready to wait on God for His plan."

That kind of humility will bring the Church back into the center of God's will and global plan. Churches today are not experiencing the power and anointing of God in their ministries because they do not have the humility to wait on Him.

We need to recover the quiet disciplines we have lost—practices such as contemplation, fasting, listening, prayer, Scripture memory, meditation, silence, submission and reflection.

So little of evangelical Christian work is done in total dependence upon the living God. Like our brothers and sisters in that big church, we have devised methods, plans and techniques to "do" God's work. Those involved apparently sense no need to pray or be filled with the Holy Spirit to do the work of Jesus.

How far we have drifted from the faith of the apostles and the prophets! What a tragedy when the techniques of the world and its agents are brought into the sanctuary of God. Only when we are emptied of our own self-sufficiency can God use us. When a church or a mission board spends more time in consultation, planning and committee meetings than in prayer, it is a clear indication the members have lost touch with the supernatural and have ended up, as Watchman Nee describes it, serving the house of God and forgetting the Lord Himself.

Part of the sin of pride is a subtle but deep racism. As I travel, I often hear innocent-sounding questions such as, "How do we know that the national church is ready to handle the funds?" or "What kind of training have the national missionaries had?"

So long as such questions are based on a sincere desire for good stewardship, they are commendable, but I have found that sometimes the intent of these questions is less honorable. If we're satisfied that a certain national missionary is truly called to the Gospel and the Lord is asking us to stand with him, then we need to trust God and be willing to give just as we would to another brother in our own culture. To try to control the ministry overseas from our foreign-based mission board is, without our realizing it, an extension of colonialism. It can humiliate and weaken the national missionaries in the long run.

Christians need to learn that they are not giving *their* money to national workers. They are giving *God's* money to *His* work overseas.

We are driven by powerful egos always to be right. We are often slaves to a strong tendency to "have it our way." All of these are manifestations of pride, the opposite of the servanthood and humble sacrifice commanded by Christ. We need instead to follow Christ's example and set our hearts on serving Him by serving our fellow Asian children of God. Making a sacrifice for one of the unknown brethren—supporting his work to a strange people in a strange place, using methods that are a mystery to you—does take humility. But supporting the national brethren begins with this kind of commitment to humility and continues in the same spirit. Sadly, our pride too often stands in the way of progress.

Unbelief

I have come to see that many evangelical Christians do not really believe the Word of God, especially when it talks about hell and judgment. Instead, they selectively accept only the portions that allow them to continue living in their current lifestyles.

C.S. Lewis, that great British defender of the faith, wrote, "There is no doctrine which I would more willingly remove from

Christianity than this [hell]. . . . I would pay any price to be able to say truthfully, 'All will be saved.' "[1]

But Lewis realized that was neither truthful nor within his power to change.

It is painful to think about hell and judgment. I understand why preachers do not like to talk about it, because I don't either. It is so much easier to preach that "God loves you and has a wonderful plan for your life," or to focus on the many delightful aspects of "possibility thinking" and the "word of faith" that brings health, wealth and happiness. The grace and love of God are pleasant subjects, and no one more beautifully demonstrated them than our Lord Jesus. Yet in His earthly ministry, He made more references to hell and judgment than He did to heaven. Jesus lived with the reality of hell, and He died on Calvary because He knew it was real and coming to everyone who doesn't turn to God in this life.

Believers are willing to accept the concept of heaven, but many look the other way when they come to passages in the Bible about hell. If we knew the horrors of the potential judgment that hangs over us—if we really believed in what is coming—how differently we would live.

Why aren't Christians living in obedience to God? Because of their unbelief.

Why did Eve fall into sin? Because she did not truly believe in the judgment—that death really would come if she ate what God forbade. This is the same reason many continue in lives of sin and disobedience.

The crises facing our world today are only a slap on the wrist compared to what lies ahead—wars, recessions, disease and natural calamities. But God is withholding judgment now to give us time to repent.

Unfortunately for millions in our world, it will be too late unless we can reach them before they slip off the edge into eternal darkness.

For years I struggled with making this a reality in our meetings. Finally I found a way.

I ask my listeners to hold their wrists and find their pulse. Then I explain that every beat they feel represents the death of someone who has died and plunged into eternity without ever hearing the Good News of Jesus Christ even once.

"What if one of those beats represented your own mother?" I ask. "Your own father, your spouse, your child . . . you yourself?"

We say we believe it—but what are we doing to act on that faith? Without works, faith is dead.

No one should die without hearing about the Lord Jesus. To me this is an atrocity much worse than the death camps of Hitler's Germany or Stalin's Russia. If only a small percentage of the people who claim to be born-again Christians were to support the work of national missionaries, we could have literally hundreds of thousands of evangelists reaching the lost villages of Asia. When we look at the unfinished Great Commission and compare it to our personal lifestyles—or to the activity calendars of our churches and organizations—how can we explain our disobedience? We must see a great repentance from the sin of our unbelief in God's judgment.

C.T. Studd, the famous British athlete and founder of W.E.C., was one who gave up all his achievements in this life for Christ's sake. He was challenged to his commitment by a tract written by an atheist. That article in part said:

> Did I firmly believe, as millions say they do, that the knowledge and practice of religion in this life influences destiny in another, religion would mean to me everything.

I would cast away earthly enjoyments as dross, earthly cares as follies, and earthly thoughts and feelings as vanity. Religion would be my first waking thought, and my last image before sleep sank me into unconsciousness. I would labor in its cause alone. I would take thought for the morrow of eternity alone. I would esteem one soul gained for heaven worth a life of suffering. . . . I would strive to look upon eternity alone, and on the immortal souls around me, soon to be everlastingly happy or everlastingly miserable. I would go forth to the world and preach to it in season and out of season, and my text would be, WHAT SHALL IT PROFIT A MAN IF HE GAIN THE WHOLE WORLD AND LOSE HIS OWN SOUL?[2]

Worldliness

Once, on a 2,000-mile auto trip across the American West, I made it a point to listen to Christian radio all along the way. What I heard revealed much about the secret motivations that drive many Christians. Some of the broadcasts would have been hilarious if they weren't exploiting the gullible—hawking health, wealth and success in the name of Christianity.

Some speakers offered holy oil and lucky charms to those who sent in money and requested them. One said he would mail holy soap that he had blessed. If used with his instructions, the soap would wash away bad luck, evil friends and sickness. Again he promised "plenty of money" and everything else the user wanted.

Christian magazines, TV shows and church services often put the spotlight on famous athletes, beauty queens, businessmen and politicians who "make it in the world and have Jesus too!" Today, Christian values are defined almost totally by success as it is promoted by Madison Avenue advertising.

But in contrast, John says in his first epistle, "Do not love the world or the things in the world. If anyone loves the world, the love of the Father is not in him. For all that is in the world— the lust of the flesh, the lust of the eyes, and the pride of life—is not of the Father but is of the world. And the world is passing away, and the lust of it; but he who does the will of God abides forever" (1 John 2:15–17).

The typical media testimony goes something like this: "I was sick and broke, a total failure. Then I met Jesus. Now everything is fine; my business is booming, and I am a great success."

It sounds wonderful. Be a Christian and get that bigger house and a boat and vacation in the Holy Land. But if that were really God's way, it would put believers living in anti-Christian countries in a pretty bad light. Their testimonies often go something like this:

"I was happy. I had everything—prestige, recognition, a good job, and a happy wife and children. Then I gave my life to Jesus Christ. Now I am in prison, having lost my family, wealth, reputation, job and health.

"Here I live, lonely, deserted by friends. I cannot see the face of my wife and dear children. My crime is that I love Jesus."

Christian martyrs have written their names on every page of history. In the former Soviet Union, Ivan Moiseyev was tortured and killed within two years of meeting Jesus. In China, Watchman Nee spent 20 years in prison and finally died in bondage.

When Sadhu Sundar Singh, born and raised in a rich Sikh's home in Punjab, became a Christian, his own family tried to poison him and banished him from their home. He lost his inheritance and walked away with one piece of clothing on his body. Yet, following his Master, he made millions truly rich through faith in Christ.

Today's national workers often suffer for their commitment also. Coming from non-Christian backgrounds, they often are literally thrown out of their homes, lose their jobs and are beaten and chased from their villages when they accept Christ. They faithfully serve Christ daily, suffering untold hardships because Jesus promised His followers, "In the world you will have tribulation; but be of good cheer, I have overcome the world" (John 16:33). What He promised were trials and tribulations. But they can face them because they know He already has won the battle.

God does promise to meet our physical needs. And He does, indeed, bless His children materially. But He blesses us for a purpose—not so we can squander those resources on ourselves but so we can be good stewards, using our resources wisely to win the lost to God's saving grace.

I have spoken in churches that have no missionary program of any kind, and this in spite of having a pastor known to be an excellent Bible teacher with a love for people. How is this possible?

"Evangelical Christianity," commented Tozer prophetically before his death, "is now tragically below the New Testament standard. Worldliness is an accepted part of our way of life. Our religious mood is social instead of spiritual."

The Church Jesus called out of this world to be separated unto Himself has, to a great extent, forgotten her reason for existence. Her loss of balance is seen in the current absence of holiness, spiritual reality and concern for the lost. Substituted for the life she once knew are teaching and reaching for prosperity, pleasure, politics and social involvement.

The further our leaders wander from the Lord, the more they turn to the ways of the world. Many churches have become like secular clubs with softball teams, golf lessons, schools and exercise classes to keep people coming to their buildings and giving them their tithes.

What would Jesus do if He walked into our churches today?

I am afraid He would not be able to say to us: "You have kept the faith, you have run the race without turning left or right, and you have obeyed My command to reach this world." I believe He would go out to look for a whip, because we have made His Father's house a den of robbers. If that is so, then we must repent of our sin of pride, unbelief and worldliness while there is still time. The hour is too desperate for us to continue to deceive ourselves. If this Gospel is to be preached in all the world in our lifetime, we need more than revival or reformation. We must cry out for a Christian, heaven-sent revolution.

11

WHY SHOULD I MAKE WAVES?

By the end of 1981, Gospel for Asia appeared to be gaining acceptance. Many were beginning to share in the ministry of equipping national missionaries to evangelize in their own countries.

As Gisela and our office staff in Dallas worked to assign our new sponsors to national missionaries, I felt led of the Lord to plan a road tour of 14 Texas towns to meet personally with new supporters. Calling ahead, I introduced myself and thanked the people for taking on the sponsorship of a national missionary.

I was stunned by the response. Most of the people had heard me on the radio and appeared thrilled with the idea of meeting me. In every town, someone offered me lodging and made arrangements for me to speak in small house meetings and churches. People were referring to me in a new way—as the president and director of an important missionary organization. Far from being pleased, I was more terrified than ever—afraid that I would fail or be rejected.

With the meetings booked solid and the publicity out, an unreasonable fear took over. A weariness settled upon me. As the day for my departure came closer, I looked for excuses to cancel or postpone the whole venture.

"My family and the office need me more," I argued. "Besides, I'll be driving alone. It's dangerous and difficult—I should really wait until someone can go with me."

Just when I had almost talked myself out of going, the Lord spoke to me in an unmistakable voice during my personal morning devotion. As on other occasions, it was just as if He were in the room with me.

"My sheep hear My voice," said the Lord, using His words from John 10, "and I know them and they follow Me: My sheep follow Me because they know My voice."

I did not need an interpretation; the message was clear. The trip had been ordained by Him. He had arranged it and opened the doors. I needed to picture myself as a little lamb and follow my Shepherd over the miles. He would go ahead of me to every church and every home in which I would stay.

It turned out to be a heavenly two weeks. In every home and church, I had delightful fellowship with our new friends—and we added a number of supporters as a result.

The church in Victoria, Texas, was almost my last stop, and the Lord had a surprise waiting for me there.

My presentation went nicely. I showed the GFA slides and made an impassioned plea for our work. I explained the philosophy of our ministry, giving the biblical reasons why the people of Asia are lost unless national missionaries go to them.

Suddenly, I felt the Spirit prompting me to talk about the dangers of the humanist social gospel. I paused for the briefest moment, then went on without mentioning it. I just did not have the courage. I might make enemies everywhere. People would think I was an unloving fool, a spoiler of Christian work who did not even care about the hungry, naked, needy and suffering. Why should I make waves? I managed to get through my presentation, and feeling relieved, I opened up the meeting to questions.

But the Holy Spirit was not about to let me off the hook.

From far in the back of the room, a tall man—at least "six foot three" as they say in Texas—came walking steadily up the aisle, looking bigger and bigger as he came closer to me. I did not know who he was or what he had to say, but I felt instinctively that God had sent him. When he reached me, he wrapped a huge arm around my skinny shoulders and said some words I can still hear ringing today: "This man here, our brother, is fearful and afraid to speak the truth . . . and he's struggling with it." I felt my face and neck getting hot with guilt. How did this big cowboy know that? But it got worse, and I was about to see proof that the Spirit of the living God was really using this tall Texan to deliver a powerful confirmation and rebuke to me.

"The Lord has led you in ways others have not walked and shown you things others have not seen," he went on. "The souls of millions are at stake. You must speak the truth about the misplaced priority on the mission field. You must call the Body of Christ to return to the task of preaching salvation and snatching souls from hell."

I felt like a zero, yet this was undeniably a miraculous prophecy inspired by God, confirming both my disobedience and the very message God had called me to preach fearlessly. But my humiliation and liberation were not over yet.

"The Lord has asked me," the tall man said, "to call the elders up here to pray for you that this fear of man will leave you."

Suddenly I felt like even less than a zero. I had been introduced as a great mission leader; now I felt like a little lamb. I wanted to defend myself. I did not feel as if I were being controlled by a spirit of fear; I felt that I was just acting logically to protect the interests of our mission. But I submitted anyway, feeling a little ridiculous, as the elders crowded around me to pray for an anointing of power on my preaching ministry.

Something happened. I felt the power of God envelop me. A few minutes later I got up from my knees a changed man, released from the bondage of fear that had gripped me. All doubts were gone: God had placed a burden on my life to deliver this message.

Since that day I have insisted we recover the genuine message of Jesus—that balanced New Testament message that begins not with the physical needs of people, but with sharing the Gospel of salvation.

Modern man unconsciously holds in highest regard the humanistic ideals of happiness, freedom and economic, cultural and social progress for all mankind. This secular view says there is no God, heaven or hell; there is just one chance at life, so do what makes you most happy. It also teaches that "since all men are brothers," we should work for that which contributes toward the welfare of all men.

This teaching—so attractive on the surface—has entered our churches in many ways, creating a man-centered and man-made gospel based on changing the outside and social status of man by meeting his physical needs. The cost is his eternal soul.

The so-called humanist gospel—which isn't really the "good news" at all—is called by many names. Some argue for it in familiar biblical and theological terms; some call it the "social gospel," but the label is not important.

You can tell the humanist gospel because it refuses to admit that the basic problem of humanity is not physical, but spiritual. The humanist will never tell you that sin is the root cause of all human suffering. A humanist ministry may claim to "care for the whole man," but the reality is that it provides help for only the body and soul—ignoring the spirit.

Because of this teaching, many churches and mission societies now are redirecting their limited outreach funds and personnel away from the life-changing power of the Gospel to something vaguely called "social concern." Today Christian missionaries often find themselves primarily involved in social work. This is done in the name of Jesus and supposedly is based on His command to go into all the world and preach the Gospel to every creature.

There is, of course, nothing wrong with social work when it is combined with Christ's lifesaving message of forgiveness. In fact, Jesus taught us that, as His followers, this is exactly what we are called to do. But the mission of the Church, as defined by these humanists, can be almost anything *except* winning people to Christ and discipling them.

History already has taught us that this gospel—without the blood of Christ—is a total failure. In few countries is this more apparent than in Thailand. There, after 150 years of missionaries showing marvelous social compassion, Christians still make up only two percent of the entire population.[1]

Self-sacrificing missionaries probably have done more to modernize Thailand than has any other single force. The country owes to missionaries its widespread literacy, first printing press, first university, first hospital, first doctor and almost every other benefit of education and science. In every area, including trade and diplomacy, Christian missionaries put the needs of the host nation first and helped usher in the 20th century. Meanwhile, millions have slipped into eternity without the Lord. They died more educated, better governed and healthier—but they died without Christ and are bound for eternity without God.

By contrast, I have met poor, often minimally educated, national brothers involved in Gospel work in pioneer areas.

They had nothing material to offer the people to whom they preached—no agricultural training and no medical relief or school program. But hundreds of lives were transformed, and congregations were established. What were these brothers doing right to achieve such results, while others with many more advantages had failed?

Watchman Nee, an early Chinese national missionary, put his finger on the problem in a series of lectures delivered in the years before World War II. Read some of his comments on such efforts, as recorded in the book *Love Not the World:*

When material things are under spiritual control they fulfill their proper subordinate role. Released from that restraint they manifest very quickly the power that lies behind them. The law of their nature asserts itself, and their worldly character is proved by the course they take.

The spread of missionary enterprise in our present era gives us an opportunity to test this principle in the religious institutions of our day and of our land. Over a century ago the Church set out to establish in China schools and hospitals with a definite spiritual tone and an evangelistic objective. In those early days not much importance was attached to the buildings, while considerable emphasis was placed on the institutions' role in the proclamation of the Gospel. Ten or fifteen years ago you could go over the same ground and in many places find much larger and finer institutions on those original sites, but compared with the earlier years, far fewer converts. And by today many of those splendid schools and colleges have become purely educational centers, lacking in any truly evangelistic motive at all, while to an almost equal extent, many of the hospitals exist now solely as places merely of physical and no longer spiritual healing. The men who initiated them had, by their close walk with God, held those institutions steadfastly into His purpose; but when they passed away, the institutions themselves quickly gravitated toward worldly standards and goals, and in doing so classified themselves as "things of the world." We should not be surprised that this is so.

Nee continues to expand on the theme, this time addressing the problem of emergency relief efforts for the suffering:

In the early chapters of the Acts we read how a contingency arose which led the Church to institute relief for the poorer saints. That urgent institution of social service was clearly blessed of God, but it was of a temporary nature. Do you exclaim, "How good if it had continued!"? Only one who does not know God would say that. Had those relief measures been prolonged indefinitely they would certainly have veered in the direction of the world, once the spiritual influence at work in their inception was removed. It is inevitable.

For there is a distinction between the Church of God's building, on the one hand, and on the other, those valuable social and charitable by-products that are thrown off by it from time to time through the faith and vision of its members. The latter, for all their origin in spiritual vision, possess in themselves a power of independent survival which the Church of God does not have. They are works which the faith of God's children may initiate and pioneer, but which, once the way has been shown and the professional standard set, can be readily sustained or imitated by men of the world quite apart from that faith.

The Church of God, let me repeat, never ceases to be dependent upon the life of God for its maintenance.[2]

Our battle is not against flesh and blood or symptoms of sin such as poverty and sickness. It is against Lucifer and countless demons who struggle day and night to take human souls into a Christless eternity. If we intend to answer man's greatest problem—his separation from the eternal God—with rice handouts, then we are throwing a drowning man a board instead of helping him out of the water.

A spiritual battle fought with spiritual weapons will produce eternal victories. Knowing this, Satan has woven a masterful web of appealing half-truths to confuse the Church and ensure that millions will perish without ever hearing the Gospel. Here are a couple of his more common inventions:

One, how can we preach the Gospel to a man with an empty stomach? A man's stomach has nothing to do with his heart's condition of being a rebel against the holy God. A rich American on Fifth Avenue in New York City or a poor beggar on the streets of Kathmandu are both rebels against God Almighty, according to the Bible.

I have sat on the streets of Mumbai with beggars—poor men who very soon would die. In sharing the Gospel with many of them, I told them I had no material goods to give them, but I came to offer eternal life. I began to share the love of Jesus who died for their souls, about the many mansions in my Father's house (see John 14:2) and the fact that they can go there to hunger and thirst no more. The Lord Jesus will wipe away every tear from their eyes, I said. They shall no longer be in any debt. There shall no longer be any mourning, crying or pain (see Revelation 7:16, 21:4).

What a joy it was to see some of them opening their hearts after hearing about the forgiveness of sin they can find in Jesus! That is exactly what the Bible teaches in Romans 10:17, "So then faith comes by hearing, and hearing by the word of God."

Two, social work—meeting only the physical needs of man—is mission work; in fact, it is equal to preaching. Luke 16:19–25 tells us the pitiful story of the rich man and Lazarus. Of what benefit were the possessions of the rich man? He could not pay his way out of hell. His riches could not comfort him. The rich man had lost everything, including his soul. What about Lazarus? He didn't have any possessions to lose, but he had made preparations for his soul. What was more important during their time on earth? Was it the care for the "body temple" or the immortal soul? "For what profit is it to a man if he gains the whole world, and is himself destroyed or lost?" (Luke 9:25).

If we could spend only one minute in the flames and torment of hell, we would see how unloving the so-called "gospel" is that prevails in much of missions today. It is a crime against lost humanity to go in the name of Christ just to do social work and neglect calling men to repent—to give up their sin—and follow Christ with all their hearts.

Do not be deceived by the devil's ploys. Time is short, and thousands are perishing daily without Christ. Unless we return to the biblical balance—to the Gospel of Jesus as He Himself proclaimed it, we will lose this generation to Satan.

12

HOPE HAS MANY NAMES

The question is, what is biblical balance? What *does* the Bible say about social justice and compassion? What does it teach us concerning the Church's role in these matters?

A good place to start is to look at Christ's example, how He lived on this earth.

When Jesus came, He not only fed people's souls with the truths of heaven and Him as the Bread of Life, but He filled their stomachs with fish and bread and wine as well.

He opened not only the eyes of people's hearts to see the truth, but also their physical eyes, restoring their sight so they could see the world around them.

He strengthened the faith of the weak, while strengthening the legs of the lame.

He who came to breathe eternal life into a valley of dry, dead souls also breathed life into the widow's son, raising him up once more (see Ezekiel 37:1–9; Luke 7:11–15).

We see that with Jesus, it was not one or the other—it was *both*, and both for the glory of God.

This example of ministry carries all throughout the Bible. Look back through the Old Testament and you will see a strong emphasis placed on compassion toward the needy and social justice for the downtrodden and poor. God demanded the care and protection of all those who were oppressed (see Leviticus 19:18; Isaiah 1:17, 58:10–11), and some of the most terrible judgments fell upon the cities of Sodom and Gomorrah for the way that they exploited the poor and needy. Yet God's mercy for the weak never trumped His concern for their sin.

In Matthew 22:38–40, Jesus clearly marked the Christian's social responsibility when He said that loving God is the first and greatest commandment and "the second is like it: 'You shall love your neighbor as yourself.' On these *two* commandments hang all the Law and the Prophets" (emphasis mine).

All the Law and Prophets are summed up in *both*—loving God and loving others. It was not one or the other—but again *both*, for the glory of God. We cannot say we love others if we ignore their spiritual needs. Just the same, we cannot say we love others if we ignore their physical needs. Jesus came for both.

Indeed, it was physical suffering that brought many to call upon Him as the Savior of their soul.

In John 20:30–31 we are told, "Jesus did many other signs in the presence of His disciples . . . that you may believe that Jesus is the Christ, the Son of God, and that believing you may have life in His name." The Gospels show that it was the sick, the demon-possessed, the hungry and the poor who came to Jesus and whose lives were changed by His healing touch. Jesus Himself declared that He had come to preach the Good News to the poor, the prisoners, the blind and the oppressed (see Luke 4:18).

Through the many who were healed from horrible diseases and set free from satanic bondage, Jesus showed Himself as the only One able to save their souls from sin and death. The mercy ministries Jesus did were not an end in themselves, but were rather a means for people to understand the Father's love. And it is the same today.

ABOVE: **For too many** Dalit children in South Asia, the innocence of childhood is lost in poverty, child labor and exploitation. The problem of illiteracy—90 percent in some areas—leaves little room for hope.

LEFT: **Through Gospel for Asia's Bridge of Hope Program,** children from Dalit and other low-caste communities receive quality instruction and personal attention from staff who love them.

BELOW: **This tasty and nutritious meal** provided through GFA's Bridge of Hope Program may be the only meal of the day for some of these children.

ABOVE: **A GFA-supported pastor** and the people of his village rejoice together as the first drops of water flow out of this newly installed "Jesus Well." By God's grace, both the well and the pastor will be faithful witnesses of Jesus to this village for years to come.

RIGHT: **Leprosy is a fearsome disease** because of the disfigurement it causes and the social stigma it carries. Following the example of Jesus, GFA-supported workers reach out with compassion to those affected by this dreaded disease.

ABOVE: **The majority of young people** who enroll in a GFA-supported Bible college come with a burden to take Christ's love to the poor and needy people of their world. They receive three years of spiritual and practical training to equip them to effectively serve the Lord on the mission field.

LEFT: **During Bible college,** students learn the necessity of seeking God's will in prayer for everything in their life and ministry.

As I mentioned in the previous chapter, we must not misunderstand or replace evangelism with social action. The Great Commission is not a mandate for political liberation. The making of disciples is our aim and goal in all things. But this in no way means that we do not care about the physical suffering of those whom we seek to serve.

Our spirits, which are eternal and infinitely more precious than the whole physical world, are contained in perishable, physical bodies. And throughout Scripture, we see that God used the felt needs of the body to draw people to Himself.

And truly, the needs of suffering men, women and children in this world are great—especially in Asia.

Calcutta alone is home to more than 100,000 street children who know neither mother nor father, love nor care. They are not just numbers or statistics—they are real children. Though nameless and faceless on the streets where they live, each one was created with love and is known by God.

It is doubtful they've ever held a toothbrush or a bar of soap; they've never eaten an ice-cream cone or cradled a doll. The child laborers of South Asia toil in fireworks, carpet and match factories; quarries and coal mines; rice fields, tea plantations and pastures. Because they are exposed to dust, toxic fumes and pesticides, their health is compromised; their bodies are crippled from carrying heavy weights. Some are bonded laborers, enslaved to their tasks by family poverty.

According to the International Labour Organization, this is life for an estimated 122 million children in Asia-Pacific.[1] In the Indian state of Tamil Nadu, 9-year-old Lakshmi works in a factory as a cigarette roller. She tells her sister's story, giving us a glimpse into their world:

My sister is ten years old. Every morning at seven she goes to the bonded labor man, and every night at nine she comes home. He treats her badly; he hits her if he thinks she is working slowly or if she talks to the other children, he yells at her, he comes looking for her if she is sick and cannot go to work. I feel this is very difficult for her.

I don't care about school or playing. I don't care about any of that. All I want is to bring my sister home from the bonded labor man. For 600 rupees I can bring her home—that is our only chance to get her back.

We don't have 600 rupees . . . we will never have 600 rupees [the equivalent of US$14].[2]

The hopeless situation facing Lakshmi's family is, tragically, a very common one among the Dalits, also known as the "Untouchables." For 3,000 years, countless millions of Untouchables in South Asia have suffered oppression, slavery and countless atrocities. They are trapped in a caste system that denies them adequate education, safe drinking water, decent-paying jobs and the right to own land or a home. Segregated and oppressed, Dalits are frequently the victims of violent crime.

In recent years, there has been a growing desire for freedom among Dalits and other low-caste groups that face similar repressive treatment. The turning point came on November 4, 2001, when tens of thousands of Dalits gathered for one of the most historic meetings of the 21st century, publicly declaring their desire to follow a faith of their own choosing.

Since that event, the Lord has led us to tangibly express His love to Dalit and low-caste families in a unique way: *by reaching out to their children.*

Gospel for Asia's Bridge of Hope Program is designed to rescue children in Asia from a life of poverty and hopelessness by helping to provide them an education and introducing them to the love of God. Through this effort, entire communities are being transformed.

Today more than 75,000 children are enrolled in hundreds of Bridge of Hope centers, and the program continues to grow. One of these centers is located in the village of a worker named Samuel.

Samuel had no idea that the group of 35 Dalit and low-caste children attending would make such a remarkable difference in his ministry. But one little first-grade boy in his center was about to show him otherwise.

Nibun's mother had been ill with malaria for a long time, and her death seemed inevitable. But Nibun had a little seed of hope in his heart—God's Word. Bible stories were a regular part of the Bridge of Hope curriculum at the center, and like many other children, Nibun would come home and narrate every story he had heard to his family.

One night, as Nibun and his family sat together beside his mother's bed, he told them how Jesus raised a widow's son from the dead. It became a turning point in all their lives.

"That night, after hearing this story," Nibun's father later shared, "I could not sleep. This story was burning in my heart again and again."

Nibun's father sought out Samuel the next morning. After hearing more about Jesus and His offer of salvation, the man asked the pastor to come and pray for his wife. "I believe Jesus will heal my wife just as He did the widow's son," he affirmed.

Nibun's mother, though weak in body, shared the same confidence: "My son talks about Jesus many times in our home. I believe Jesus will heal me."

Samuel laid hands on the dying woman and prayed for the Lord to raise her up; then he returned to his home.

The next day he saw Nibun and asked how his mother was doing.

"My mommy is walking around," he reported happily, "and this morning she prepared breakfast for us!"

When Samuel arrived at Nibun's house, he found a family transformed both physically and spiritually.

From the very beginning of Gospel for Asia, we have taken every opportunity to share the love and hope found in Jesus, especially in the most poor and needy communities. The most tangible way we have found to bring hope to desperately poor families is to help provide an education for their children, which often equals freedom in many of these nations. In fact, one of the reasons why so many children and their families stay enslaved as bond-laborers is the simple fact that they cannot read the contract made between them and their loaner. Because of illiteracy, they are blindly taken advantage of and cheated out of not just money and time, but their futures.

It is the love of Christ that constrains us to reach out in this way, knowing that each child and his family are precious in the sight of God.

Let me tell you an experience I had in the beginning stages of this ministry to the Dalits that propelled us to move forward with GFA's Bridge of Hope Program.

It was while sleeping in the early hours of the morning that I had a dream. I was standing in front of a vast wheat field, looking out upon a harvest that was clearly ripe. I stood there for a while, overwhelmed at the size of the harvest. The field continued for what seemed like millions of endless acres for as far as the eye could see.

As I stood there watching the golden wheat sway in the breeze, I got this sudden understanding that I was looking out upon the harvest that Jesus spoke of in John 4 and Matthew 9. It was as though the Lord was telling me that this harvest was free for the taking, much as Psalm 2 tells us to ask for the nations and He will give them to us.

Overcome with excitement, I ran toward the field. But as I drew nearer, I was stopped. I couldn't go any farther. There was a wide, gaping river in between the harvest field and myself, a river so deep and raging that I dared not step closer or try to cross. I had not seen it from where I stood before, but now I did.

My heart broke. I was only able to look at the harvest, unable to embrace it. I stood there weeping, feeling so helpless and full of despair.

All of a sudden there appeared before me a bridge reaching from one side of the vast river to the other. It was not a narrow bridge but was very broad and so huge.

As I watched, the bridge became completely filled with little children from all over Asia—poor, destitute Dalit children, like those I'd seen on the streets of Bombay, Calcutta, Dakar, Kathmandu and other Asian cities.

I woke up from my dream and realized that the Lord was speaking to me about something so significant: that if we follow His instruction, we will see these endless millions of Untouchables experience God's love.

I shared this dream with my colleagues, and we realized that God had given us this call to bring hope to the children of Asia. Miraculously, this has been happening. God has been faithful to carry out the plans that He placed in our hearts.

When national workers first went into communities in one mission field to share the Gospel, they were strongly opposed. But when these brothers began to set up Bridge of Hope centers for the children, they were welcomed in a new light.

Within time, dozens of Bridge of Hope centers were started in that region. Less than a year later, 37 fellowships were started. And it all began with the little children learning about Jesus, going home and telling their parents; then miracle after miracle began to transpire!

Nibun's father speaks for many parents when he says, "I thank God for this center and pray that He will use it to bring His light into many homes, just as He has done in our family."

Gospel for Asia's Bridge of Hope Program shows what can happen when Gospel proclamation and compassion ministry are kept in their proper balance. The same transforming love of God is at work in other Gospel for Asia ministries that introduce Christ to people through ministering to a felt need. Today we support special ministries among widows and street children, in leprosy colonies and slums, and many fellowships have been started among these needy people.

Many people are surprised to hear that leprosy is still a problem in the 21st century. It is true that this terrible skin disease is easily treated, but the world's poor typically do not have access to modern medicine. As a result, thousands of people in South Asia suffer needlessly from leprosy's devastating, disfiguring effects. And as in biblical times, they are usually pushed out of their communities and forced to live out their days in slum colonies along with others with the same disease.

When Jiva, one of the national missionaries we support, first witnessed someone cleaning the wounds of a leprosy patient, he thought to himself, *I could do a work like that. That would be a great thing in my life.*

Most of us would turn our eyes away from the repulsive sight of decaying flesh. Instead, Jiva found himself wanting to wash and bandage the mutilated hands and feet of these people.

This desire grew in his heart, and he began asking the Lord for an opportunity to take care of these precious people.

Jiva went on to pioneer a vibrant leprosy ministry. Today, we support dozens of national workers who serve people with leprosy. They visit leprosy colonies regularly to treat wounds, distribute medication and help in other practical ways. With each wound they dress, our workers pour on the healing balm of Christ's love and tell of His saving grace.

If you could visit one of these communities on a Sunday morning, you would see something astonishing: patients in all stages of the disease, gathered together under a tree or tent, singing and worshiping the Lord. Their faces beam with joy as they clap the stubs of their hands together to the rhythm of the music. These people have been transformed from the inside by the power of God. It happened through a touch of love.

Another desperate need in South Asia, especially for Dalits, is safe drinking water. Often, the only available water for cooking and drinking is the polluted, stagnant pond used for bathing, washing dishes, watering livestock and who knows what else. You can imagine how this contaminated water affects their health—how many sicknesses they suffer, how many of their children die.

By God's grace, Gospel for Asia has helped to provide "Jesus Wells" for thousands of needy communities. Every well includes a plaque inscribed with the words from Jesus: "Whoever drinks of this water will thirst again, but whoever drinks of the water that I shall give him will never thirst. But the water that I shall give him will become in him a fountain of water springing up into everlasting life" (John 4:13–14).

The free gift of clean water, available to everyone in the community, and Christ's gracious words of invitation testify of His love to all passersby. The wells showcase His faithfulness, too. During a hot summer in one region, every other well in the area dried up, but amazingly the Jesus Well did not! In another location, the new Jesus Well was the only one around that yielded sweet water; all the other wells in the area were salty.

Many people, after sampling the fresh, clean water of a Jesus Well and seeing the plaque, actually seek out the local GFA-supported pastor or worker. They have many questions: "What does 'Jesus Well' mean? What is written on the slab? What do these words mean?" Their questions open the door for a spiritual conversation to take place, a new friendship to be forged. In this way, the Holy Spirit draws thirsty inquirers toward Christ, the source of living water.

The Lord willing, as we move forward with a deep conviction to see the Great Commission truly fulfilled, we will see millions come to know the Lord. As we respond to their physical needs in the name of Jesus, they will hear the Good News of forgiveness from sin and redemption through the death and resurrection of the Lord Jesus Christ, and entire communities will be blessed.

When all is said and done, the bottom line must be "the poor have the gospel preached to them" (Matthew 11:5). If that is not done, we have failed.

13

ENEMIES OF THE CROSS

The indigenous missionary movement, the best hope for the unreached nations, is not going unchallenged. Revivals of traditional religions, the growth of secular materialism including communism, and the rise of cultural and nationalist barriers are all united in opposition to Christian mission activity.

Yet the love of God can penetrate even this host of barriers.

"I was brought up in a home where we worshiped many gods," says Masih, who for years sought spiritual peace through self-discipline and religious meditation as required by his caste. He even became a spiritual leader in his village but couldn't find the peace that his heart longed for.

"One day I received a Gospel tract and read about the love of Jesus Christ. I answered the offer on the leaflet and enrolled in a correspondence course to learn more about Jesus. On January 1, 1978, I gave my life to Jesus Christ. My life was completely transformed."

When his parents realized their son had become a follower of Christ, they began a campaign of persecution. To escape, Masih went to a city to search for a job. For six months he worked in a factory and meanwhile joined a local group of believers. Through their encouragement, he enrolled in a Bible school and began to study God's Word.

During his three years of study, he made his first trip home. "My father sent a telegram asking me to come home," Masih recalls. "He said he was 'terribly ill.' When I arrived, my family and friends asked me to renounce Christ. When I didn't, much persecution followed, and my life was in danger. I had to flee."

Returning to school, Masih thought God would lead him to minister to some distant mission field. He was shocked at the answer to his prayers.

"As I waited on the Lord, He guided me to go back and work among my own people," he says. "He wanted me to share the love of God through Christ with them, like the healed demoniac of Gadara whom He sent back to his own village."

Today, Masih is involved in church planting in his home city and surrounding villages, working in a basically hostile environment.

Although Masih has not had to pay the ultimate price to win his people to Christ, every year many Christian missionaries and ordinary believers in Asia and around the world are killed for their faith. The total number of Christian martyrs in the past century is estimated at 45 million, undoubtedly more than the total killed during the preceding 19 centuries of Church history.[1]

Religiosity—The Enemy of the Truth

Revivals of traditional religions are occurring all over Asia. Although few countries have gone the route of Iran—where a religious revival of Islam actually toppled the state—religious factionalism is a major problem in many countries.

When government, media and educational institutions are taken over by atheistic materialists, most nations experience a great backlash. As traditional religious leaders are finding out, it is not enough to drive Western nations out. Secular humanists are in firm control of most Asian governments, and many traditional religious leaders miss the power they once exercised.

At the grassroots level, traditional religion and nationalism often are deliberately confused and exploited by political leaders for short-term gain. In the villages, traditional religions still have a powerful hold on the minds of most people. Almost every village or community has a favorite deity—there are 330 million gods in the Hindu pantheon alone. In addition, various animistic cults, which involve the worship of powerful spirits, are openly practiced alongside many of these religions.

Into these regions, God is calling national missionaries to take the Good News to millions who have never before heard it. Their ministries are reminiscent of the Apostle Paul's, who wrote, "I have made it my aim to preach the gospel, not where Christ was named, lest I should build on another man's foundation, but as it is written: 'To whom He was not announced, they shall see; And those who have not heard shall understand'" (Romans 15:20–21).

The Spirit of the Antichrist

But the enemies of the cross include more than just traditional religionists. A new force, even more powerful, is now sweeping across Asia. It is what the Bible calls the spirit of the Antichrist—the new religion of secular materialism. Often manifested as some form of communism, it has taken control of governments in a number of countries, including Myanmar (Burma), Cambodia, China, Laos, North Korea and Vietnam. Even in those Asian nations with democracies like India and

Japan, it has gained tremendous political influence in various noncommunist forms.

Modern Asia, in the great cities and capitals where secular humanism reigns supreme, is controlled by many of the same drives and desires that have dominated the West for the past 100 years. The temples of this new religion are atomic reactors, oil refineries, hospitals and shopping malls. The priests are most often the technicians, scientists and military generals who are impatiently striving to rebuild the nations of Asia in the image of the industrial West. The shift of political power in most of Asia has gone toward these men and women who promise health, peace and prosperity without a supernatural god—for man himself is their god.

In one sense, secular humanism and materialism are correct in diagnosing traditional religion as a major source of oppression and poverty throughout Asia. But humanism, insofar as it offers a worldly and scientific method to solve the problems of mankind without God, makes itself the mortal enemy of *all* theistic religion. As a result of this growing scientific materialism, strong secularist movements exist in every Asian nation. They are united in seeking to eliminate the influence of all religion—including Christianity—from society.

The Anti-Christian Pressure of the World— The Culture

If traditional religions represent spiritual opposition to Christianity, then secular humanism is an attack of the flesh. That leaves only one enemy to discuss, the anti-Christian pressure of the world. This final barrier to Christ, and still probably the strongest of all, is the culture itself.

When Mahatma Gandhi returned to India from years of living in England and South Africa, he quickly realized the "Quit India" movement was failing because its national leadership was not willing to give up European ways. So even though he was Indian, he had to renounce his Western dress and customs; otherwise, he would not have been able to lead his people out from under the British yoke. He spent the rest of his life learning how to become an Indian again—in dress, food, culture and lifestyle. Eventually he gained acceptance by the common people of India. The rest is history. He became the father of my nation, the George Washington of modern India.

The same principle holds true of mission efforts. When people in the West are approached by yellow-robed Krishna worshipers—with their shaved heads and prayer beads—they reject the foreign religion immediately. In the same way, people from Eastern cultures reject Christianity when it comes in Western forms.

Have Asians rejected Christ? Not really. In most cases they have rejected only the trappings of Western culture that have fastened themselves onto the Gospel. This is what the Apostle Paul was referring to when he said he was willing to become "all things to all men" in order that he might win some.

Sadhu Sundar Singh, a pioneer national missionary evangelist, used to tell a story that illustrates the importance of presenting the Gospel in culturally acceptable terms.

A high-caste Hindu, he said, had fainted one day from the summer heat while sitting on a train in a railway station. A train employee ran to a water faucet, filled a cup with water and brought it to the man in an attempt to revive him. But in spite of his condition, the man refused. He would rather die than accept water in the cup of someone from another caste.

Then someone else noticed that the high-caste passenger had left his own cup on the seat beside him. So he grabbed it, filled it with water and returned to offer it to the panting heat victim who immediately accepted the water with gratitude.

Then Sundar Singh would say to his hearers, "This is what I have been trying to say to missionaries from abroad. You have been offering the water of life to the people of India in a foreign cup, and we have been slow to receive it. If you will offer it in our own cup—in an indigenous form—then we are much more likely to accept it."

When Asians share Christ with other Asians in a culturally acceptable way, the results are startling. One national worker we support in South Asia, Jager, has reached 60 villages with the Good News and established 30 churches in a difficult area. He has led hundreds to find the joy of knowing Christ. On one trip, I went out of my way to visit Jager and his wife. I had to see for myself what kind of program he was using.

Imagine my surprise when I found Jager was not using any special technology at all—unless you want to call the motor scooter and tracts that we supplied "technology." He was living just like the people. He had only a one-room house made of mud. The kitchen was outside, also made of mud—the same stuff with which everything else is constructed in that region. To cook the food, his wife squatted in front of an open fire just like the neighboring women. What was so remarkable about this brother was that everything about him and his wife was so truly native. There was absolutely nothing foreign.

I asked Jager what kept him going in the midst of such incredible challenge and suffering. He replied, "Waiting upon the Lord." I discovered he spent two to three hours daily in prayer, reading and meditating on the Bible. This is what it takes to win people for Christ.

Jager was led to Christ by another national missionary, who explained the living God to Jager. He told of a God who hates sin and became a man to die for sinners and set them free. This was the first time the Gospel was ever shared in his village, and Jager followed the man around for several days.

Finally, he received Jesus as his Lord and was disowned by his family. Overjoyed and surprised by his newfound life, he went about distributing Christian literature from village to village, telling about Jesus. In the end, he sold his two shops. With the money he earned, he conducted evangelistic meetings in local villages.

This is a man of the culture, bringing Christ to his own people in culturally acceptable ways. The support Asians need from the West, if we are to complete the work Christ has left us, must go to recruit, equip and send out more national workers like him.

The challenge of Asia cries out to us. The enemies of the cross abound, but none of them can stand against the power of Jesus' love. The problems we face are indeed great, but they can be overcome through the dedicated ministry of national missionaries.

14

A GLOBAL VISION

Should all foreign missionaries pull out of Asia forever? Of course not. God still sovereignly calls Western missionaries to do unique and special tasks in Asia, as He does in other locations. But we must understand that when it comes to nations in which Western missionaries are no longer able to serve as past eras allowed, the priority must then be to support the efforts of indigenous missionaries through financial aid and intercessory prayer.

As gently as I can, I have to say that anti-Western prejudice is running high in most of Asia. In fact, this is a section I write with the greatest fear and trembling—but these truths must be said if we are to accomplish the will of God in the Asian mission fields today.

"There are times in history," writes Dennis E. Clark in *The Third World and Mission,* "when however gifted a person may be, he can no longer effectively proclaim the Gospel to those of another culture. A German could not have done so in Britain in 1941 nor could an Indian in Pakistan during the war of 1967, and it will be extremely difficult for Americans to do so in the Third World of the 1980s and 1990s."[1] This is much more true—and the situation is even worse—today.

I am not calling for an end to denominational mission programs or the closing down of the many hundreds of Western-style missions, but I am asking us to reconsider the missionary policies and practices that have guided us for the past 200 years. As a general rule, for the following reasons, I believe it is wiser to support national missionaries in their own lands than to send Western missionaries.

One, it is wise stewardship. In most cases, missionaries in South Asia are able to provide for their family and ministry expenses on around US$10 a day. Outside of the ministry expenses included, this is generally the same per capita income of the community to whom they are ministering.

Western missionaries, however, are faced with many additional costs. Before even reaching the mission field, they incur the costs of their cross-cultural and linguistic training, which runs into many thousands of dollars. Then there is the cost to transport the family and their possessions overseas. For the cost of a single airplane ticket from New York to Kathmandu, a national missionary already on the field can support his family and minister for months.

Once at their destination, Western missionaries will typically require some sort of Western-style housing and English-language schools for their children. Western missionaries frequently face pressure to maintain a semblance of Western-style living, especially if their children attend private schools alongside the sons and daughters of international businessmen and diplomats. Hence, the cost of food, clothing and private transportation can be high. National missionaries, on the other hand, live in villages on the same level as others in the community whom they are seeking to reach for Christ.

Western missionaries also are faced with visa and other legal fees, insurance, extra medical care, import duties and requirements to pay taxes in their home countries. The host government may require foreign missionaries to meet special tax or reporting requirements, usually with payments required. Finally, there are the costs of furlough travel, communications with donors and imported entertainment such as English-language books and DVDs, none of which is part of the national missionary's lifestyle.

The result of all this is that Western missionaries typically need several times more money for their support than does a national missionary.

During a consultation on world evangelism in the 1990s, Western missionary leaders called for 200,000 new missionaries by the year 2000 just to keep pace with their estimates of population growth. The cost of even that modest missionary force would have run into multiplied billions of dollars annually. And populations continue to grow. Unless we take these facts into account, we will lose the opportunity of our age to reach untold millions with the Gospel. Today it is outrageously extravagant to send Western missionaries overseas unless there are compelling reasons to do so.

Two, in many places the presence of Western missionaries perpetuates the myth that Christianity is the religion of the West. Bob Granholm, former executive director of Frontiers in Canada, states, "While the current internationalization of the missionary task force is a very encouraging development, it is often wiser to not have a Western face on the efforts to extend the Kingdom."

Roland Allen says it better than I in his classic book, *The Spontaneous Expansion of the Church:*

> Even if the supply of men and funds from Western sources was unlimited and we could cover the whole globe with an army of millions of foreign missionaries and establish

stations thickly all over the world, the method would speedily reveal its weakness, as it is already beginning to reveal it.

The mere fact that Christianity was propagated by such an army, established in foreign stations all over the world, would inevitably alienate the native populations, who would see in it the growth of the denomination of a foreign people. They would see themselves robbed of their religious independence, and would more and more fear the loss of their social independence.

Foreigners can never successfully direct the propagation of any faith throughout a whole country. If the faith does not become naturalized and expand among the people by its own vital power, it exercises an alarming and hateful influence, and men fear and shun it as something alien. It is then obvious that no sound missionary policy can be based upon multiplication of missionaries and mission stations. A thousand would not suffice; a dozen might be too many.[2]

Jesus set the example for indigenous missionary work. The Lord became one of us in order to win us to the love of God. He knew He could not be an alien from outer space so He became incarnated into our bodies.

"As the Father has sent Me," He said, "I also send you" (John 20:21). For any missionary to be successful, he, like Jesus, must identify with the people he plans to reach. Because Westerners usually cannot do this, they are ineffective. We cannot maintain a Western lifestyle or outlook and work among the poor of Asia.

A friend of mine who heads a missionary organization similar to ours recently told me the story of a conversation he had with some African church leaders.

"We want to evangelize our people," they said, "but we can't do it so long as the white missionaries remain. Our people won't listen to us. The communists and the Muslims tell them all white missionaries are spies sent out by their governments as agents for the capitalistic imperialists. We know it isn't true, but newspaper reports tell of how some missionaries are getting funds from the CIA. We love the American missionaries in the Lord. We wish they could stay, but the only hope for us to evangelize our own country is for all white missionaries to leave."

There was a time when Western missionaries needed to go into these countries in which the Gospel was not preached. But now a new era has begun, and it is important that we officially acknowledge this. God has raised up indigenous leaders who are more capable than outsiders to finish the job.

This does not mean we do not appreciate the legacy left to us from Western missionaries. We praise God for the tremendous contribution Western missionaries made in many Two-Thirds World countries where Christ had never before been preached. Through their faithfulness, many were won to Jesus, churches were started and the Scriptures were translated. Their disciples are today's national missionaries.

Three, Western missionaries, and the money they bring, compromise the natural growth and independence of the national Church. I once met with a missionary executive of one of the major U.S. denominations. He is a loving man whom I deeply respect as a brother in Christ. He heads the colonial-style extension of his denomination into Asia, and we talked about mutual friends and the exciting growth that is occurring in the national churches of India. We shared much in the Lord. I quickly found he had as much respect as I did for the Indian brothers God is choosing to use in India today. Yet he would not support these men who are so obviously anointed by God.

"Our policy," he admitted without shame, "is to use the nationals only to expand churches with our denominational distinctives."

The words rolled around in my mind, "use the nationals." This is what colonialism was all about, and it is still what the neocolonialism of most Western missions is all about. With their money and technology, many organizations are simply buying people to perpetuate their foreign denominations, ways and beliefs.

In Thailand, a group of indigenous missionaries was "bought away" by a powerful Western parachurch organization. Once effectively winning their own people to Christ and planting churches in the Thai way, their leaders were given scholarships to train in the United States. The foreign organization provided them with expense accounts, vehicles and posh offices in Bangkok.

What price did these indigenous missionary leaders pay? They must use foreign literature, films and the standard method of this highly technical American organization. No consideration is being made of how effective these tools and methods will be in building the Thai Church. They will be used whether they are effective or not because they are written into the training manuals and handbooks of this organization.

After all, the reasoning of this group goes, these programs worked in London and Los Angeles—they must work in Thailand as well!

This kind of thinking is the worst neocolonialism. To use God-given money to hire people to perpetuate our ways and theories is a modern method of old-fashioned imperialism. No method could be more unbiblical.

The sad fact is this: God was already doing a wonderful work in Thailand by His Holy Spirit in a culturally acceptable way. Why didn't this Western group have the humility to bow before the Holy Spirit and say, "Have Thine own way, Lord"?

Often we become so preoccupied with expanding our own organizations that we do not comprehend the great sweep of the

Holy Spirit of God as He has moved upon the peoples of the world. Intent upon building "our" churches, we have failed to see how Christ is building "His" Church in every nation. We must stop looking at the lost world through the eyes of our particular organization.

Four, Western missionaries cannot easily go to the countries where most so-called "hidden people" live. More than 2 billion of these people exist in our world today. Millions upon millions have never heard the Gospel. We hear many cries that we should go to them, but who will go?

Of the more than 300,000 North American and European missionaries now actively commissioned, fewer than 10,000 are working among totally unreached peoples.[3] The vast majority are working among the existing churches or where the Gospel already is preached.

The reason, of course, is that the hidden people almost all live in countries closed or severely restricted to American and European missionaries. Fortunately, the national missionary can still go to the nearest hidden people group.

One particular people group, for example, lives in a very remote part of the Himalayan Mountains, a six-day journey by foot from the nearest village. Anyone wanting to be "the beautiful feet upon the mountains, bringing the Good News" (see Isaiah 52:7) to these people would face a long, hard hike! Moreover, the group is highly protective of their culture and quite closed to outsiders of any kind. It took a huge sacrificial effort on the part of two national missionaries to show these precious people how much Christ loved them.

This is how it happened. The two young men had a desire to share Jesus with this remote community, but when they reached the remote area, the people wouldn't let them in. The missionaries went to the village leader and asked what they needed to do in order to be allowed to live among his people. The leader suggested they become porters and serve the community. So they did. They would trek six days down the treacherous mountain to the nearest village. There they would gather supplies and then laboriously journey back up the mountain with the supplies tied on their backs. The round-trip took 15 days, and they did this once a month. For the other 15 days per month, they were allowed to live with the people, and soon the hearts of the villagers warmed to these dedicated servants and their message of hope. As a result of the faithfulness of these two brothers, a worshiping community was started among these people.

Migrant workers in far-off lands—such as the 700,000 Nepalis employed in Malaysia—must not be forgotten either. Certainly a Nepali can go to Malaysia with the Gospel more easily than someone from the West. And who better to take Christ's love to these homesick people than a fellow countryman? A few years ago, I learned of some young Nepali missionaries who did this very thing. They obeyed Christ's call to leave their mountainous homeland for the flatlands of Malaysia. There they will be able to share Christ, not only among the Nepali workers, but to a diverse multinational migrant population.

Unlike the Western missionary, the national missionary can reach the hidden peoples and can preach, teach and evangelize without being blocked by most of the barriers that confront Westerners. As a native of the country or region, he knows the cultural taboos instinctively. He can move around freely and is accepted in good times and bad as one who belongs.

Right now, national workers are seeing thousands turn to Christ in revival movements on every continent. Hundreds of new congregations are being formed every week by national missionaries in the Two-Thirds World!

15

"I Became One Among Them"

When we think about the awesome challenge of Asia, it is not too much to ask for a new outpouring of workers to reach these nations for Christ. Tens of thousands of national workers are being raised up by the Lord in all of these Two-Thirds World nations right now. They are Asians, many of whom already live in the nation they must reach or in nearby cultures just a few hundred miles from the villages to which they will be sent by the Lord.

The situation in world missions is depressing only when you think of it in terms of 19th-century Western colonialism. Think about it. During the colonial rule, it was impossible for Western missionaries to even imagine reaching all the thousands of distinct cultural groups in the colonies. They focused their attention on the major cultural groups in easy-to-reach centers of trade and government. Even the few churches that were established among the dominant cultural groups appeared weak. They were directly controlled by foreigners, and not surprisingly, the masses shunned these strange centers of alien religion, much as most Westerners avoid "Krishna missions" or "Islamic missions" in the West today.

For Western missionaries, the possibility of going beyond the major cultural groups to the masses of people in rural areas, ethnic subcultures and minorities—reaching out to the unfinished task—would have been generations away with these methods. If the actual task of world evangelization depended on the "sending of the white missionary," obeying the Great Commission truly would become more impossible every day. The withdrawal of foreign missionaries freed the Gospel from the Western traditions that they had unwittingly added to it, and churches of Asia have now emerged on fire. The indigenous missionary movement is growing, ready today to complete the task.

But, one may ask, are national workers prepared to carry on *cross-cultural* ministry? The answer is yes, and with great effectiveness! Most of the national missionaries we support are involved in some form of cross-cultural missions. They may have to learn a new language, adopt different dress or adjust to dietary customs. However, because the cultures are frequently neighbors or share a similar heritage, the transition is much easier than it would be for someone coming from the West. Almost anyone in India, Bangladesh, Myanmar, Bhutan, Thailand and Sri Lanka can be trained relatively quickly to cross-minister in a neighboring culture.

Please don't misunderstand me. I am not saying that it is always easy and pain-free for national missionaries to serve cross-culturally. There is often a very high price the missionary must pay, as in the case of Dayal.

After attending Bible college, Dayal had prayed about where the Lord was calling him to serve. When his leader suggested this one particular region, he was dismayed, but he agreed to pray about it. Soon, he had confirmation that this was God's choice for him.

He did not have to cross any national borders to reach his new mission field, but it felt to him like the other side of the world.

On the day of his arrival, he was invited to dinner. There he got his first dose of culture shock. In a pot before him sat a boiled goat head, its eyeballs staring out at him from its boiled skull. Beyond the pot of goat, Dayal's hosts sat, watching him.

Dayal managed to swallow some bites of goat that night, to the satisfaction of his hosts. But the food was just the beginning of the loss he would experience—death to all that was familiar and comfortable.

His new home was beautiful, surrounded by forested hills and rice paddies. But behind the beauty were deep needs rooted in spiritual darkness. The people were animists who worshiped the sun and moon and feared the violent gods of the rivers and storms. Among the population, immorality, alcoholism and family violence were rampant.

The first two months were an intense struggle. He lost weight. He was homesick and lonely. Twice he packed his bags. Finally, Dayal laid his heart open before the Lord.

"This is too difficult," he prayed. "I want to go back, because things are not good here." The response he received from the Lord marked a turning point.

"If everything were good here," Dayal sensed God speaking, "why would you need to come here? It is because things are not good—because things are not convenient—that I called you here. I am giving you 2 million people."

Dayal's own life changed that day. He began to view the challenges with a perspective that was bigger than his own. And as he persevered in his ministry work, things began to happen.

Among the fruit of Dayal's ministry are hundreds of young disciples, both men and women, many of whom have started congregations in other areas.

He also launched the first-ever Gospel radio broadcast in the local language. The radio signal raced through the region, and just a month later, Dayal received an earnest letter from a village 45 kilometers away.

"For the first time in our lives, we heard a radio broadcast in our own language," the letter read. "We are 13 people here, ready to know Jesus more. We don't know what to do. Something is happening in our hearts; please come and help us."

Dayal and another believer traveled by bicycle and reached the village in the afternoon.

The group of 13 became the first congregation started through Dayal's ministry. Soon, four other congregations were established, along with two "radio churches" made up of listeners who spread the word about the broadcast to their relatives and neighbors.

"I have become one among them," Dayal explains. "They don't see me as an outsider anymore because I visit with them, I eat with them, I dance with them, I pray with them. They have even given me a new last name."

Although Dayal's mission field lay hidden within his own country, other missionaries are called to cross national boundaries to bring Christ to new areas. For example, a handful of Bible college graduates from Myanmar responded to the Lord's call to "go" to a neighboring country that until recently was completely closed to the Gospel. Their leader instructed them to assimilate into the culture and learn how to communicate the Gospel effectively in their new homeland. If any of them wanted to marry, he was to marry a godly local woman and raise his family there. In other words, this was not a short-term mission trip; these young men were sent off with "one-way tickets."

A couple of years later, one of these missionaries sent a request for what sounded like a huge amount of money to construct a church building there in that country. Naturally, his leader inquired, "Why so much money? What sort of building are you planning to construct?" The missionary answered back, "Just a normal building, except that it needs to be large enough to hold 700 worshipers." In just two years, this one missionary had already established a congregation of more than 500 believers, and the Lord was adding to their numbers daily. In building this large church, he was merely planning ahead for the expected growth.

In talking about hidden, hard-to-reach people groups, I have yet to mention the largest and most inaccessible group of all. Do you know who they are?

The correct answer is, women.

Think about it. In many Eastern and Middle-Eastern cultures, women live very secluded lives. They are far less likely than men to be able to read and write. They often have little or no freedom to take part in public life. They are not generally allowed to even talk to men outside their immediate family.

These restrictions make it next to impossible for a male missionary to share about Christ with a woman. *How then will she hear?*

There is only one solution. We must help train and send women missionaries. Unlike men, women have easy access to other women in these cultures.

Gospel for Asia today supports thousands of women missionaries who are taking the Gospel where men can't. They visit homes during the day, spending time with the women in the household, building friendships, praying for their needs and sharing the Gospel in sensitive ways. Everywhere they go, doors and hearts open.

These women are rigorously prepared for their unique role in the ministry. In addition to receiving biblical training, they also learn how to teach literacy, basic health and child care and other practical subjects to help needy women on their mission fields.

Women missionary teams are going to some very difficult places. One such place is a group of small islands off the coast of India. The only way to make a living on these remote, primitive islands is by fishing, but unfortunately over the years, tigers have killed off large numbers of men as they go out on the waters for a catch. As a result, the islands are filled with grieving widows, many with small children, struggling to survive, surrounded by wild beasts.

Several women's teams have chosen to live on these islands so that they can minister to the widows. These sisters go house to house, visiting the shut-ins, praying for the sick and sharing the Word of God. They also have started literacy, basic health care and vocational training classes to help the widows provide for themselves and take care of their children. The love of Christ being poured out through these women missionaries is attracting many to their Savior.

Far from these swampy tropical islands, another woman missionary serves the Lord high up in the Himalayas. Her country is completely off-limits to outside Christian workers, yet we are able to support national workers there, including Sister Tashi.

One particular village has a reputation for its violent opposition to Christianity. At various times, different male missionaries attempted to visit the village, but they experienced nothing but threats and abuse from the townspeople. Fully aware of the risk, Tashi said yes when the Lord called her to go to this village and show them His love.

She approached the village with an offer to start a free tutoring center for their children. Because most of the people were poor, eking out a living off the land, they were excited about her offer and said they would discuss it among themselves and inform her of their decision.

Within a week, Tashi visited the village again, talked to more families, and came to the conclusion that, whatever the cost, she would start a tutoring center there. By God's grace, the villagers agreed, and as a result, she was able to move into the village.

In the beginning, just six children came for tutoring, but every month the number increased. Sister Tashi gave the children baths, taught them action songs, told them short stories from the Bible and helped them learn basic things like the alphabet and numbers, etc. She also taught them how to pray. Every two months, she would hold a meeting for the parents to counsel them on family matters and share the Good News.

After a while, a few of the villagers who did not have children started to oppose her work, knowing that she was a Christian. But the majority stood by Tashi's side, saying, "If you want Sister Tashi to leave our village just because she is a Christian, then first find another sincere, caring, loving and committed woman like her from some other faith who will take care of our children like she is doing."

After much heated debate, the opposing individuals were overruled. From then on, the ministry flourished. Tashi started a Sunday school, then a weekly prayer meeting, then a Bible study. As more people started showing interest in Jesus, another missionary joined her in the work. There is now a worshiping community in this place, and the entire village is being transformed by Christ's love.

In almost every country of Asia, men and women missionaries are effectively winning their people to Christ using culturally acceptable methods and styles. Although persecution against Christians is on the rise in many of these nations, still the work goes on. The commission of the Church will not cease until Jesus returns.

We are all called to be involved by sharing prayerfully and financially in the great work that lies ahead. As we do this, perhaps we will see together the fulfillment of that awesome prophecy in Revelation 7:9–10:

> And behold, a great multitude which no one could number, of all nations, tribes, peoples, and tongues, standing before the throne and before the Lamb, clothed with white robes, with palm branches in their hands, and crying out with a loud voice, saying, "Salvation belongs to our God who sits on the throne, and to the Lamb!"

This prediction is about to come true. Now, for the first time in history, we can see the final thrust taking place as God's people everywhere unite to make it possible.

What should intrigue us is the way the indigenous missionary movement is flourishing without the help and genius of our Western planning. The Holy Spirit, when we give Him the freedom to work, prompts spontaneous growth and expansion. Until we recognize the indigenous missionary movement as the plan of God for this period in history, and until we are willing to become servants to what He is doing, we are in danger of frustrating the will of God.

16

THE CHURCH'S PRIMARY TASK

These are the wonderful, final days of Christian history. Now is the time for the whole family of God to unite and share with one another as the New Testament Church did, the richer churches giving to the poorer.

As I sit on platforms and stand in pulpits, both in the East and in the West, I am speaking on behalf of the national brethren. God has called me to be the servant of the needy brothers who cannot speak up for themselves.

As I wait to speak, I look out over the congregation, and I often pray for some of the workers by name. Usually I pray something like this: "Lord Jesus, I am about to stand here on behalf of Thomas John and P.T. Steven tonight. May I represent them faithfully. Help us meet their needs through this meeting."

Of course, the names of the national workers change each time. But I believe the will of God will not be accomplished in our generation unless this audience and many others like it respond to the cry of the lost. Each of us must follow the Lord in the place to which He has called us—the national evangelist in his land and the sponsors in their lands. Some obey by going; others obey by supporting; some by praying. Even if you cannot go to Asia, you can fulfill the Great Commission by helping send national workers to the pioneer fields.

This and many other similar truths about missions are no longer understood by the people of God. Preaching and teaching about missions have been lost in most of our churches. The sad result is seen everywhere. Most believers no longer can define what a missionary is, what he or she does or what the work of the Church is as it relates to the Great Commission.

A declining interest in missions is the sure sign that a church and people have left their first love. Nothing is more indicative of the moral decline than Christians who have lost the passion of Christ for a lost and dying world. Many churches have slipped so far from biblical teaching that Christians cannot explain why the Lord left us here on earth.

All of us are called for a purpose. Some years ago when I was in North India, a little boy about eight years old watched me as I prepared for my morning meditations. I began to talk to him about Jesus and asked him several questions.

"What are you doing?" I asked the lad.

"I go to school," was the reply.

"Why do you go to school?"

"To study," he said.

"Why do you study?"

"To get smart."

"Why do you want to get smart?"

"So I can get a good job."

"Why do you want to get a good job?"

"So I can make lots of money."

"Why do you want to make lots of money?"

"So I can buy food."

"Why do you want to buy food?"

"So I can eat."

"Why do you want to eat?"

"To live."

"Why do you live?"

At that point, the little boy thought for a minute, scratched his head, looked me in the face and said, "Sir, why do I live?" He paused a moment in mid-thought, then gave his own sad answer, "To die!"

The question is the same for all of us: Why do we live?

What is the basic purpose of your living in this world, as you claim to be a disciple of the Lord Jesus Christ? Is it to accumulate wealth? Fame? Popularity? To fulfill the desires of the flesh and of the mind? To somehow survive and, in the end, to die and hopefully go to heaven?

No. The purpose of your life as a believer must be to obey Jesus when He said, "Go ye into all the world, and preach the gospel. . . ." That is what Paul did when he laid down his arms and said, "Lord, what do You want me to do?"

Jesus called two of His first disciples, Simon and Andrew, with these words, "Follow Me, and I will make you become fishers of men" (Mark 1:17). Do you remember what these two brothers were doing when Jesus spoke these words to them? They were fishing. These were professional fishermen who exhausted themselves daily in hopes of a big catch, because their livelihood depended on it.

Knowing what fish meant to these men, Jesus used a fishing metaphor to explain God's higher purpose for their lives. "As valuable as these fish may be to you," Jesus essentially was saying, "the souls of men are infinitely more valuable to Me."

Jesus calls each of us in the same way, although the metaphor of our heart may be different: "As valuable as (fill in the blank) may be to you, the souls of men are infinitely more valuable to Me. Follow Me."

If all of your concern is about your own life, your job, your clothes, your children's good clothes, healthy bodies, a good education, a good job and marriage, then your concerns are no different from a pagan.

When Jesus was here on earth, His goal was to do nothing but the will of His Father. Our commitment must be the same. Jesus no longer is walking on earth, but we are. We are His body; He is our head. That means our lips are the lips of Jesus. Our hands are His hands; our eyes, His eyes; our hope, His hope. My wife and children belong to Jesus. My money, my talent, my education—all belong to Jesus.

So what is His will? What are we to do in this world with all of these gifts He has given us?

"As the Father has sent Me, I also send you," are His instructions. "Go therefore and make disciples of all the nations, baptizing them in the name of the Father and of the Son and of the Holy Spirit, teaching them to observe all things that I have commanded you; and lo, I am with you always, even to the end of the age" (John 20:21; Matthew 28:19–20).

Every Christian should know the answers to the following three basic questions about missions in order to fulfill the call of our Lord to reach the lost world for His name.

One, what is the primary task of the Church? Each of the four Gospels gives us a mandate from our Lord Jesus, the mission statement of the Church, known as the Great Commission. See Matthew 28:18–20, Mark 16:15–16, Luke 24:47 and John 20:21.

The Great Commission reveals the reason God has left us here in this world, the main activity of the Church until Jesus returns as the King of kings to gather us to Himself. He desires us to go everywhere proclaiming the love of God to a lost world. This task involves more than handing out leaflets, holding street meetings or showing compassionate love to the sick and hungry, although these may be involved. But the Lord wants us to continue as His agents to redeem and transform the lives of people. Disciple-making, as Jesus defined it, involves the long-term process of establishing local congregations. These congregations then become agents for positive change in their communities.

Note too that the references to the Great Commission are accompanied by promises of divine power. This is obviously a task for a special people who are living intimately enough with God to discern and exercise His authority.

Two, who is a missionary? A missionary is anyone sent by the Lord to establish a new Christian witness where such a witness is yet unknown. Traditionally-defined missionary activity usually involves leaving our own immediate culture for another, taking the Gospel to people who differ in at least one aspect—such as language, nationality, race or tribe—from our own ethnic group.

For some reason, many Westerners have come to believe that a missionary is only someone from the West who goes to Asia, Africa or some other foreign land. Not so. When a former upper-caste person crosses the subtle caste lines of India and works among low-caste people, he is a missionary just as much as a person who goes from Detroit to Dhaka.

Christians in the West must abandon the totally unscriptural idea that they should support only white missionaries from their own country. Today it is essential that we support missionaries going from India to Mongolia, from one island of the Philippines to another or from Korea to China.

Unless we abandon the racism implied in our unwritten definition of a missionary, we will never see the world reached for Christ. Although governments may close the borders of their countries to Western missionaries, they cannot close them to their own people. The Lord is raising up national missionaries right now, but they cannot do it alone. In the words of Paul the Apostle, "How shall they hear without a preacher? And how shall they preach *unless they are sent?*" (Romans 10:14–15 emphasis mine).

Three, where is the mission field? One of the biggest mistakes we make is to define mission fields in terms of nation states. These are only political boundaries established along arbitrary lines through wars or by natural boundaries such as mountain ranges and rivers.

A more biblical definition conforms to linguistic and tribal groupings. Thus, a mission field is defined as any cultural group that does not have an established group of disciples. The Arabs of New York City, for example, or the people of the Hopi Indian tribe in Dallas are unreached people groups in the United States. More than 10,000 such hidden people groups worldwide represent the real pioneer mission fields of our time.

They will be reached only if someone from outside their culture is willing to sacrifice his or her own comfortable community to reach them with the Gospel of Christ. And to go and do so, that person needs believers at home who will stand behind him with prayers and finances. The indigenous missionary movement in Asia—because it is close at hand to most of the world's unreached peoples—can most easily send the workers. But they cannot always raise the needed support among their destitute populations. This is where Christians elsewhere can come forward, sharing their abundance with God's servants in reaching the unreached.

Missionary statesman George Verwer believes most Christians are still only "playing soldier." Verwer writes,

> Some missionary magazines and books leave one with the impression that worldwide evangelization is only a matter of time. More careful research will show that in densely populated areas the work of evangelism is going backward rather than forward.
>
> In view of this, our tactics are simply crazy. Perhaps 80 percent of our efforts for Christ—weak as they often are—still are aimed at only 20 percent of the world's population. Literally hundreds of millions of dollars are poured into every kind of Christian project at home, especially buildings, while only a thin trickle goes out to the regions beyond. Half-hearted saints believe by giving just a few hundred dollars they have done their share. We all have measured ourselves so long by the man next to us we barely can see the standard set by men like Paul or by Jesus Himself.
>
> During the Second World War, the British showed themselves capable of astonishing sacrifices (as did many other nations). They lived on meager, poor rations. They cut down their railings and sent them for weapons manufacture. Yet today, in what is more truly a (spiritual) World War, Christians live as peacetime soldiers. Look at Paul's injunctions to Timothy in 2 Timothy 2:3–4: "Thou therefore endure hardness, as a good soldier of Jesus Christ. No man that warreth entangleth himself with the affairs of this life; that he may please him who hath chosen him to be a soldier." We seem to have a strange idea of Christian service. We will buy books, travel miles to hear a speaker on blessings, pay large sums to listen to a group singing the latest Christian songs—but we forget that we are soldiers.[1]

You may never be called personally to reach the hidden peoples of Asia, but through soldier-like suffering at home, you can make it possible for millions to hear overseas.

Today I am calling on Christians to give up their stale Christianity, use the weapons of spiritual warfare and advance. We must stop skipping over the verses that read, "If anyone desires to come after Me, let him deny himself, and take up his cross, and follow Me," and "So likewise, whoever of you does not forsake all that he has cannot be My disciple" (Matthew 16:24; Luke 14:33).

Were these verses written only for the national missionaries who are on the front lines being stoned and beaten and going hungry for their faith? Or were they written only for certain believers comfortably going through the motions of church, teaching conferences and concerts?

Of course not. These verses apply equally to Christians in Bristol, Boston and Bombay.

Day after day I continue with this one message: Godly national missionaries are waiting to go to the next village with the Gospel, but they need your prayer and financial support. We are facing a new day in missions, but it requires the cooperation of Christians in both the East and West.

17

THE VISION OF ASIA'S NEED

Many Christians concerned about missions have grown up hearing the classic approach: "Send our own people." They have never been asked to consider alternatives better suited to changed geopolitical conditions. It is hard for some to hear me reinterpret the stories told by Western missionaries of hardship and fruitless ministry as indicators of outdated and inappropriate methods.

But the biggest hurdle for most Westerners is the idea that someone from somewhere else can do it better. So naturally they have questions about our methods and safeguards for financial accountability.

On one of my trips, I was invited to meet with the mission committee of a church that supported more than 75 Western missionaries. After I shared our vision for supporting national missionaries, the committee chairman said, "We have been asked to support national missionaries before, but we haven't found a satisfactory way to hold these nationals accountable for either the money we send or the work they do." I sensed he spoke for the entire committee.

I could hardly wait to respond. This issue of accountability is the objection most often raised about supporting national missionaries to the Two-Thirds World, and I can understand why. Indeed, I agree it is extremely important that there be adequate accountability in every area of ministry. Good stewardship demands it.

So I detailed how we handle the subject.

"In order to make people accountable, we need some norm by which to measure their performance," I said. "But what criteria should we use? Would the yearly independent audit missionaries submit be adequate to see that they handled money wisely?"

I raised other questions. "What about the churches they build or the projects they have undertaken? Should they be judged according to the patterns and goals that other mission headquarters or denominations prescribe? What about the souls they've won and the disciples they've made? Does any denomination have criteria to evaluate those? How about criteria to evaluate their lifestyle on the field or the fruit they produce? Which of these categories should be used to measure national missionary accountability?"

Those who had been leaning back in their chairs were now leaning forward. I had laid a foundation for a thought I was sure they hadn't considered before. I continued:

"Do you require the Western missionaries you send overseas to be accountable to you? What criteria have you used in the past to account for the hundreds of thousands of dollars you have invested through the missionaries you support now?"

I looked to the chairman for an answer. He stumbled through a few phrases before admitting they never had thought of requiring "their" missionaries to be accountable, nor was this ever a concern to them.

"The problem," I explained, "is not a matter of accountability but one of prejudice, mistrust and feelings of superiority. These are the issues that hinder love and support for our brothers in the Two-Thirds World who are working to win their own people to Christ." I followed with this illustration:

"Three months ago, I traveled to one South Asian country to visit some of the brothers we support. In one country, I met a Western missionary who had for 14 years been developing some social programs for his denomination. He had come to this country hoping he could establish his mission center, and he had been successful. As I walked into his mission compound, I passed a man with a gun, sitting at the gate. The compound was bordered by a number of buildings with at least half-a-dozen imported cars. The staff members were wearing Western clothes, and a servant was caring for one of the missionary children. The scene reminded me of a king living in a palace with his court of serfs caring for his every need. I have, in 18 years of travel, seen this scene repeated many times.

"From conversation with some of the national missionaries," I continued, "I learned that this missionary and his colleagues did live like kings with their servants and cars. They had no contact with the poor in the surrounding villages. God's money is invested in missionaries like these who enjoy a lifestyle they could not afford back home—a lifestyle of a rich man, separated by economy and distance from the national missionaries walking barefoot, poorly dressed even by their own standards and sometimes going without food. These nationals, in my opinion, are the real soldiers of the cross. Each one of the brothers we support in that country has established a fellowship in less than 12 months, and some have started a dozen in three years.

"You are seeking accountability from national missionaries, accountability that is required for you to give them support? Remember that Jesus said, 'For John came neither eating nor drinking, and they say, "He has a demon." The Son of Man came eating and drinking, and they say, "Look, a glutton and a winebibber, a friend of tax collectors and sinners!" But wisdom is justified by her children' (Matthew 11:18–19).

"Fruit," I pointed out, "is the real test. 'By their fruits you will know them,' Jesus said (Matthew 7:20). Paul told Timothy to do two things regarding his life. And these two things, I believe, are the biblical criteria for accountability. He told Timothy to watch his own life and to care for the ministry that was committed to him. The life of the missionary is the medium of his message."

Much time had passed, yet the room remained quiet. I sensed I had their permission to continue.

"You asked me to give you a method to hold national missionaries accountable. Gospel for Asia does have definite procedures to ensure that we are good stewards of the monies and opportunities the Lord commits to us. But our require-ments and methods reflect a different perspective and way of doing missions.

"First, Gospel for Asia assumes that those who are called are called to serve and not to be served. The missionaries we support walk before the millions of poor and destitute in Asia with their lives as an open testimony and example. They breathe, sleep and eat conscious of the perishing millions the Lord com-mands us to love and rescue."

Then I explained how God is reaching the lost, not through programs but through individuals whose lives are so committed to Him that He uses them as vessels to anoint a lost world. So we give top priority to how the missionaries and their leaders live. When we started to support one brother, he lived in two small rooms with concrete floors. He, his wife and four children slept on a mat on the floor.

That was four years ago. On a recent visit to India, I saw him living in the same place, sleeping on the same mat even though his staff had grown from 30 to 349 workers. He handles hundreds of thousands of dollars to keep this enormous ministry going, yet his lifestyle has not changed. The brothers he has drawn into the ministry are willing to die for Christ's sake because they have seen their leader sell out to Christ just as the Apostle Paul did.

"In the West, people look to men with power and riches. In Asia, our people look for men like Gandhi who, to inspire a following, was willing to give up all to become like the least of the poor. Accountability begins with the life of the missionary.

"The second criterion we consider," I explained, "is the fruitfulness of that life. Our investment of money shows in the result of lives changed and churches established. What greater accountability can we require?

"When Western missionaries go into Two-Thirds World countries, they are able to find nationals to follow them. But these nationals too often get caught up in denominational distinctives. Like produces like. Missionary leaders from denominations who fly into these countries and live in five-star hotels will draw to themselves so-called national leaders who are like themselves. Then, unfortunately, it is the so-called national leaders who are accused of wasting or misusing great amounts of money, while they have often merely followed the example provided by their Western counterparts."

Again I addressed the chairman: "Have you studied the lives and ministries of the Western missionaries you support? I believe you will find that very few of them are directly involved in preaching Christ but are doing some sort of social work. If you apply the biblical principles I have outlined, I doubt you would support more than a handful of them."

Then I turned and asked the committee members to assess themselves.

"If your life is not totally committed to Christ, you are not qualified to be on this committee. That means you cannot use your time, your talents or your money the way you want to. If you do and still think you can help direct God's people to reach a lost world, you mock God Himself. You have to evaluate how you spend every dollar and everything else you do in the light of eternity. The way each one of you lives is where we begin our crusade to reach the lost of this world."

I was gratified to see that the Lord spoke to many of them. There were tears and a feeling of Christ's awareness among us. This had been a painful time for me, and I was glad when it was over. But I needed to be faithful to God's call on my life to share the vision of Asia's lost souls with the affluent Christian brothers and sisters who have it in their power to help.

18

"LORD, HELP US REMAIN TRUE TO YOU"

Yes, today God is working in a miraculous way. Thousands of believers around the world are catching the vision of God's third wave in missions and are helping to support the work of national missionaries. Many pastors, church leaders, former missionaries and Christian broadcasters in the West are also unselfishly lending their support. But I believe this is only a foretaste of what will happen in the days ahead.

In addition to our sponsors and donors, hundreds of volunteers are coordinating efforts at the grassroots level. This network of local workers is making a tremendous contribution in fulfilling the Great Commission. They represent Gospel for Asia at conferences and distribute literature to friends. They show GFA videos and share what the Lord is doing through national missionaries with churches, Sunday schools, home Bible studies, prayer meetings and other Christian gatherings. By recruiting additional senders, they multiply what they could have given on their own.

One young volunteer was barely out of high school when she first caught the vision and began to sponsor a missionary. Then, when she discovered our Christmas Gift Catalog and saw the different ways she could be involved in giving to the work in Asia, she wrote to tell us how excited she was and how she couldn't stop telling people about it.

Next she got her church involved in the cause. "By myself there was only so much I could do. But through the junior high and college ministries, we were able to raise enough for a Jesus Well. Thank you so much for this opportunity."

I will never forget one dear retired widow whom I met on a speaking tour. Excited about how much she still could do even though she wasn't working, she pledged to help support a missionary out of her tiny Social Security check.

After six months I received a very sad letter from her. "K.P.," she wrote, "I am so privileged to be supporting a missionary. I'm living all alone now on only a fixed income. I know when I get to heaven I'm going to meet people who have come to Christ through my sharing, but I must reduce my support because my utility bills have gone up. Please pray for me that I will find a way to give my full support again."

When my wife, Gisela, showed me the letter, I was deeply touched. I called the woman and told her she need not feel guilty—she was doing all she could. I even advised her not to give if it became a greater hardship.

Two weeks later, another letter came. "Every day," she wrote, "I've been praying for a way to find some more money for my missionary. As I prayed, the Lord showed me a way—I've disconnected my phone."

I looked at the check. Tears came to my eyes as I thought how much this woman was sacrificing. She must be lonely, I thought. What would happen if she got sick? Without a phone, she would be cut off from the world. "Lord," I prayed, as I held the check in both hands, "help us to remain true to You and honor this great sacrifice."

fold before tearing

GOSPEL FOR ASIA

Dear Brother K.P., after reading *Revolution in World Missions*, I want to help national workers share Christ's love with their own people. I understand it can take up to \$360 per month to fully support one national missionary, including family support and ministry expenses.

☐ **Starting now, I will commit to _____ monthly pledge(s)** for national missions at \$30 each, for a total of \$ _____ per month. You will receive a photo and the personal information of a national missionary for each \$30 pledge to national missions.

☐ **I would like to give an additional \$5 per month** to help Gospel for Asia gain more support for national missions.

☐ **Please send me more information** about supporting national missions.

Please circle: Mr.   Mrs.   Miss   Rev.

Name _____

Address _____

City _____ State _____ Zip _____

Phone (_____) _____

Email _____

☐ **I give Gospel for Asia permission to send me emails** (i.e. field stories, urgent prayer requests, etc.).

Privacy Policy: Gospel for Asia will not sell, lease or trade your personal information.

All gifts are subject to our gift acceptance policy. | gfa.org/giftpolicy   **HB71-RB1C**

Choose the missionary you'd like to link your life with.

gfa.org/missionaries

I want to make a
DIFFERENCE!

I want to help national workers share Christ's love with their own people.

Your stamp on this card is like an
additional donation!—Bro. K.P.

fold before tearing

BUSINESS REPLY MAIL

FIRST-CLASS MAIL · PERMIT NO 1 · WILLS POINT TX

POSTAGE WILL BE PAID BY ADDRESSEE

GOSPEL FOR ASIA
1116 ST THOMAS WAY
WILLS POINT TX 75169-9911

Support national missions,
read news from the field,
or download additional
resources online at:

WWW.GFA.ORG

ABOVE: **The Asian culture of gender segregation** makes it difficult for a male missionary to reach out to women in the same way that a woman missionary easily can, by visiting with other women and sharing about Jesus. GFA has helped train and send thousands of women missionaries to tell the precious women of Asia about the love of their Savior.

BELOW: **These national missionaries** serve in the mountain regions. They must often hike dangerous mountain trails, risking their very lives, to bring the Good News to those who haven't yet heard.

ABOVE: **Film is a powerful way** to share the message of God's love with the people of Asia, especially in areas where the literacy rate is low. When a GFA-supported film team arrives in a tiny village and requests permission to show a film about Jesus, often the entire town will come out to see it. As villagers learn for the first time about Jesus' love and sacrifice, tears stream down many faces.

BELOW: **Radio is another** effective way to minister to people living in remote areas. GFA funds Gospel broadcasts in more than 100 Asian languages. In response, every year more than 1 million people write or call, asking for prayer and information about the Lord.

RIGHT: **National missionaries** must often walk 10 to 15 miles to reach the closest neighboring village. A bicycle enables them to reach many more. Gospel for Asia helps provide bicycles for national missionaries, enabling them to go farther, faster.

BELOW: **Every year,** Gospel for Asia provides the resources to print millions of pieces of literature to offer words of hope and new life in all the major languages of the Indian Subcontinent.

ABOVE: **This church building** is more than simply a worship center for believers. It also provides a place to conduct literacy classes, medical clinics and other activities that bless the entire community. New fellowships often worship in temporary shelters, exposed to summer heat, monsoon rains, overcrowding and harassment, until they are able to construct a church building of their own.

BELOW: **When a massive earthquake** struck Nepal in 2015, national missionaries in Nepal and neighboring countries rushed to provide relief and comfort to the earthquake victims. GFA was privileged to support their efforts with prayer and funds in partnership with the Body of Christ around the world.

The widow's sacrifice has inspired others in ways I never would have imagined. One woman wrote in, "When I read the story of the widow who disconnected her phone, I cried. As I cried, the Holy Spirit reminded me about my expensive coffee habit, and I knew that if this woman could go without a phone, I could go without buying lattes." A married couple responded to the widow's story by cutting off their own television service. "And what a blessing that has been," they wrote. "Not only do we have more money to give to missions, but we can be better stewards of our time."

Another gift, this time from a 13-year-old boy named Tommy, shows the same spirit of sacrifice. For more than a year, Tommy had been saving for a new bicycle for school. Then he read about the value of bicycles to national workers like Mohan and his wife from a hot, dry region in South Asia. Since 1977, Mohan had been walking in the scorching sun between villages, engaged with his wife in disciple-making through Bible classes, open-air evangelism, literature distribution, children's ministry and Bible translation. He and his family lived in one rented room and had to walk for miles or ride buses to do Gospel work. A bicycle would mean more to him than a car would mean to someone in suburban England.

But a new locally made bicycle in Asian nations, which would cost around US$100 to $200, was totally out of reach for his family's budget. What amazed me when I came to the West is that bikes here are considered children's toys or a way to lose weight. For national missionaries, they represent a way to expand the ministry greatly and reduce suffering.

When Tommy heard that national missionaries use their bikes to ride 17 to 20 miles a day, he made a big decision. He decided to give to GFA the bike money he had saved.

"I can use my brother's old bike," he wrote. "My dad has given me permission to send you my new bike money for the national missionary."

Some people find unusual ways to raise extra national missionary support. One factory worker went through all the trash cans at his workplace collecting aluminum beverage cans. Each month we would get a check from him—usually enough to help support two or more missionaries.

One pastor personally helps support several national missionaries. Like other pastors, he has been overseas to learn about the work of national missionaries. In addition to his congregation's monthly support, he has invited Gospel for Asia speakers to make several presentations at the church. As a result, several hundred families are also supporting the work of national missions. Through his influence, a number of other pastors also started to include GFA in their regular mission budgets.

One of GFA's dearest friends has been David Mains of Mainstay Ministries in Wheaton, Illinois. Through my guest visits on his radio broadcasts, sponsors have joined our family from all across the United States. David and his wife, Karen, have advised and helped us in a number of much-needed areas, including the first edition of this book.

Support for the work of Gospel for Asia has come from other Christian organizations in some unique ways. For example, early in our ministry we were invited to participate in the Keith Green Memorial Concert Tour as the official representative of Two-Thirds World missions.

Today, thanks to the Internet, people in many different countries can help support national missionaries. We stay connected with our global family through our website, social media and email. They can even join in praying with the home office staff through the wonder of internet live-streaming technology. By God's grace, Gospel for Asia's reach is becoming truly international.

Perhaps the most exciting long-range development has been a slow but steady shift in the attitude of Western mission agencies and denominations toward indigenous mission movements.

One after another, older missions and denominations have changed anti-national policies and are beginning to support indigenous missionary movements as equal partners in the work of the Gospel. The old racism and colonial mind-set are slowly but surely disappearing.

This, I believe, could have long-range impact. If older Western mission societies would use their massive networks of support to raise funding for indigenous missions, it would be possible for us and similar indigenous missionary ministries to support thousands more national workers in the Two-Thirds World.

The day of the indigenous missionary movement has come. The seeds have been planted. Ahead of us lie much cultivation and nurture, but it can happen if we will share our resources as the Apostle Paul outlined in 2 Corinthians 8 and 9. There he urges the wealthy Christians to collect monies and send support to the poor churches in order that equality may abound in the whole Body of Christ. Those who have should share with those who have not, he argues, because of Christ's example:

"For you know the grace of our Lord Jesus Christ, that though He was rich, yet for your sakes He became poor, that you through His poverty might become rich" (2 Corinthians 8:9).

There is joy and a sense of renewed purpose when we simply obey the Lord in this area of giving. One sponsor described it this way:

I already had a desire to live a simple life well below my income so I can send money back out. But as I read *Revolution in World Missions*, I came to see that I am not giving money just because it is a joy for me but because God has specifically made me this way. As of now anyway, this is a specific calling on my life and His will for me to be involved in the Great Commission—to live simply and yet still bring in an income, thereby being able to support several missionaries who will impact many lives.

I was overjoyed to realize that my desire to give was so much more important than I previously thought. I was so humbled and yet felt such a responsibility too. I never fully understood the importance of giving until I saw that I could help support a national missionary who would share the Gospel with hundreds and thousands of people. It gave me a greater dedication, devotion and joy to forsake all.

One couple caught the message and demonstrated real spiritual understanding. They wrote, "While we were reading your *SEND!* [now called *GFA World*] magazine, the Lord began to speak to us about going to Asia. As we pondered this and asked the Lord about it, He spoke again and said, 'You're not going physically, but you're going spiritually and financially.'

"Well, praise the Lord—here is our 'first trip' to Asia. Please use this money where you see the greatest need. May God's richest blessing be upon you and your ministry."

Enclosed was a check for $1,000. It was signed, "Fellow workers in Christ, Jim and Betty."

My prayer? For several hundred thousand more like Jim and Betty with the spiritual sensitivity to hear what the Lord is saying today to the Church.

CONCLUSION

How can I ever forget the summer months I spent with mission outreach teams in the region known as the "graveyard of missions"? We were driven out from many villages and stoned for preaching the Gospel. That was in 1968.

This desperately poor rural region with 100 million inhabitants is said to be one of the most unreached places in the world. Today, there is a Bible college to train and send out workers to this spiritually needy area.

Brother S. was one of the young people who attended. In these schools, the students are encouraged to pray and seek God's face as to where He wants them to go when they finish their training. While Brother S. was studying at the Bible college, he prayed that the Lord would guide him to a place where he could reach the needy and start at least one local fellowship. The Lord placed a special burden on his heart for a specific people group in this very difficult region. So after his graduation, he was sent there to serve and reach these souls for whom he had prayed.

Three years later, he had already established five churches! All this began with the transformation of one lady named M.

Over the years, M. had earned the reputation of a holy woman in her village. Many villagers became her followers and came to her for counsel. They would bring gifts and sacrifices to her because she was known for her spiritual powers. She had the reputation for doing many miracles, even causing sickness and death.

When Brother S. arrived in that area, people told him what a powerful woman M. was, with all her magical powers. But then he heard that three years before, M. had become ill and now was totally paralyzed from the neck down. This young brother realized that this situation was God's appointed opportunity for him to share Christ's love with her.

Despite the danger to his own life, Brother S. set out to visit M. and talk to her about the Lord Jesus Christ. It was only on his way that he learned more about her story. For weeks, many ritual prayers with sacrifices had been carried out for her healing. Hundreds of her followers obeyed her careful instructions to petition her favorite deities on her behalf, but nothing had healed her. Recognizing that she must be under attack from evil spirits more powerful than she could handle, she decided to approach even stronger witch doctors to conduct elaborate rituals for her healing. But again, there was no deliverance or hope.

It was at this time that Brother S. came to her area. When he arrived at her home, he began to witness to her about the Lord Jesus Christ. She listened carefully and told him, "For three years I have tried everything to appease these angry spirits. But they don't answer. And now I am confused and terribly frightened."

He asked her, "If Jesus would heal you and make you well, what would you do?" Without hesitating she replied, "If your Jesus Christ can heal me and make me well, I will serve Him the rest of my life." Brother S. further explained to her about the reality of God's love and how Jesus Christ, the only Savior, could set her free from sin and save her from entering eternity without hope.

God in His grace opened M.'s eyes to see the truth. She decided to call upon Jesus to forgive her sin and save her. Brother S. knelt beside her and prayed for Jesus to heal her. As he prayed aloud, he also fervently prayed in his heart, "Lord Jesus, this may be my only opportunity to see this entire village come to You. Please, Lord, for Your kingdom's sake, touch her and heal her. Your Word says that You will work with me, confirming Your Word, and that miracles would be a sign for these people to believe in You."

As he finished praying, the power of the Holy Spirit and the grace of God instantly touched M., and she was delivered and healed immediately. Within a few hours she was running around, shouting with joy, "Thank you, Jesus! Thank you, Jesus! Thank you, Jesus!"

Hearing the commotion, a large crowd gathered in front of the house to see what was going on. There she was, a woman who had been paralyzed for three years, now completely healed. With tears running down her face, she was praising Jesus and shouting His name. M. became the first individual in her village to believe in Jesus.

The following week, more than 20 people gave their lives to Christ. M. opened her house for these new believers to come regularly and worship the Lord Jesus Christ. Just like in Acts 19, when the Ephesian church had its beginning, all evil practices and rituals were completely eradicated, and there was a whole new beginning for this village.

Brother S. began to preach the Gospel in the neighboring villages as well, and even more people began to come to the Lord Jesus Christ.

Hearing about these events, the leaders from the Bible college asked Brother S. if he would visit other workers in the nearby regions and help them. He began to travel, and as a result of his ministry, four more congregations were established and several new mission stations opened up.

At one point, I talked with Brother S.'s leader and asked him, "What is the secret to this brother's ministry? What is it that causes the Lord to use him so effectively?" The leader replied, "His case is not an exception. Many of our brothers on the mission field are experiencing the same thing. This is harvest time."

Then he told me something about Brother S.'s life. When he was studying in our Bible college, every morning he would get up early and spend at least three hours with the Lord, on his knees in prayer and meditating on God's Word. When he graduated and went to the mission field, he didn't cut back. Instead, the amount of time he spent in prayer increased. Brother S. doesn't talk publicly about any of these things, but very quietly and humbly goes about sharing the Gospel. Through his life, hundreds are turning to Christ.

Today, hundreds of thousands of villages remain without a Christian witness in countries like Bhutan, Myanmar, Nepal—the entire subcontinent. Millions and millions wait for someone like Brother S. to come and bring the light of the Gospel.

Romans 10:13–17 says that if these multiplied millions sitting in darkness call upon the Lord Jesus Christ, they will be saved. But how can they call on Jesus if they don't believe in Him? And second, how can they believe in Jesus if no one has ever gone to tell them about Him? Finally, you and I are asked this question: How can a person like Brother S. go unless someone has *sent* him? This is the question we must answer.

Today, God is calling us to become *senders* of missionaries who are waiting to go to these unreached villages. We have a God-given privilege to link our lives with Brother S. and others like him to see our generation come to know the Lord Jesus Christ.

I encourage you to seek the Lord and see if He is asking you to pray for and help support the work of national missions. If He puts this on your heart, let us know of your decision. You will receive information about missionaries you can partner with, which will be especially helpful as you lift them up in prayer.

It can take up to $360 a month for a national missionary to be fully supported. By giving as little as $30 a month, you can help GFA support their work and send them to villages that are waiting to hear the Good News. Through your prayers and support, you can help them effectively communicate the message of Jesus and establish local churches. Normally, missionaries will start at least one fellowship their very first year on the mission field.

Suppose *you* are the one who is privileged to pray for Brother S. Someday in eternity, you will stand before the throne with him, his family—and the thousands who have come to know the Lord through his life and ministry!

Appendix One
Questions and Answers

One of the most meaningful moments in our meetings is the question-and-answer period. Many ask some very provocative questions, which shows they have been thinking seriously about the implications of the message they just heard. Some questions seek details about policies and practices on the mission field. Certain questions come up repeatedly, and the following are my responses.

QUESTION: What are the qualifications of workers you support?

ANSWER: We are looking for those who have a definite call upon their lives to go to the most unreached areas to do evangelism and start local churches. It is not a job. A hireling quits when the going gets tough. Our commitment is to help train and send out men and women who seek only God's approval and God's glory, those who will not be bought with money or seek their own, even in the work of the Lord.

They must also be people of integrity in the area of commitment to the Word of God and correct doctrine, willing to obey the Scriptures in all matters without question. They must maintain a testimony above reproach, both in their walks with the Lord and also with their families.

We look for those who are willing to work hard to reach the mission field where they are placed. Each worker is also a shepherd of the flock that the Lord raises up. He will protect these new believers and lead them into maturity in Christ through teaching God's Word and equipping them to share Christ with others.

QUESTION: To whom are national workers accountable?

ANSWER: We take several steps to ensure that accountability systems work without failure. In each area, the missionaries meet together at least once a month for a few days of fasting prayer and fellowship as they build the kingdom in their part of the field. In all cases, national missionaries are supervised by local indigenous elders under whom they work. In turn, these field leaders spend much time meeting with godly senior leaders. The senior leaders who oversee the ministry of an entire region or country are men of integrity and testimony, both in their lives and ministries, for many years.

QUESTION: Are financial records audited on the field?

ANSWER: Yes, financial records are inspected by field administrative offices to ensure that funds are used according to the purposes intended. A detailed accounting in writing is required for projects such as village crusades, training conferences and special programs. Missionary support funds are signed for and received both by the leaders and the missionaries involved, and these receipts are checked. All financial records on the field are also audited annually by independent certified public accountants.

QUESTION: How are national workers trained?

ANSWER: Missionaries are trained in Bible colleges throughout the heart of the 10/40 Window. After graduation, the students go directly to the most unreached areas of Asia to fulfill the Great Commission given by the Lord Jesus Christ.

The training for these students is intensive. Their days begin at 5 A.M. The first hour is spent in prayer and meditation on God's Word. Teaching and practical training take place throughout the remainder of the day. Around 11 P.M. their days end.

Each Friday evening is set apart for fasting and more than two hours of prayer. Every weekend the students go to the nearby unreached villages for evangelism. Usually before the end of the school year, they have started dozens of local fellowships through these weekend outreach ministries. Before they finish their three-year training, each student will have carefully read through the entire Bible at least three times.

The students spend the first Friday of every month in all-night prayer, praying especially for those in greatest need of the Gospel in their own country and abroad. Through these times of prayer, the reality of the lost world becomes very close to their hearts, as each student is given the opportunity to pray for dozens of totally unreached people groups. At the same time, each one seeks the Lord's face as to where He will have them go for ministry.

The most important part of the training is for the students to become more like Christ in their character and nature and for them to know the Lord intimately in their lives. Second, they are taught the Word of God in such a way that they are well-equipped, not only to do outreach work, but also to be effective pastors and teachers in the churches they establish. An inductive Bible study course is required for graduation. Third, during their three years, the students receive a tremendous amount of practical training for all aspects of the ministry, including personal evangelism, serving the poor, caring for the needs of widows, developing a congregation and pastoral care, to help them be effective in the work of the Lord.

QUESTION: What are the methods used by the national missionaries?

ANSWER: Although films, radio, television and the Internet are becoming more common in Asia, some of the most effective methods still sound more as if they came from the book of Acts!

The most effective evangelism is done face-to-face in the streets. Most national missionaries walk or ride bicycles between villages, much like the Methodist circuit riders rode their horses in America's frontier days. Sometimes workers arrange witnessing parades or tent campaigns and distribute simple Gospel tracts during weeklong village crusades.

Because the majority of the world's 1 billion illiterate people live in Asia, the Gospel often must be explained to them without using literature. This may be done through showing a film on the life of Jesus and using flip charts or other visual aids to communicate the Gospel.

Rugged vehicles, bicycles, film projectors, loudspeaker systems, Gospel literature and Bibles are all important tools for our missionaries that do not shock the culture. They are available in Asia and can be purchased locally without import duties. Today, these simple ministry tools are supplemented with culturally sensitive radio and television broadcasting.

QUESTION: With your emphasis on the indigenous missionary movement, do you feel there is still a place for Western missionaries in Asia?

ANSWER: Yes, there still are places for Western missionaries.

One, there are still countries with no existing church from which to draw national missionaries. Morocco, Afghanistan and the Maldive Islands come to mind. In these places, missionaries from outside—whether from the West, Africa or Asia—are a good way for the Gospel to be spread.

Two, Christians in the West have technical skills that may be needed by their brothers and sisters in Two-Thirds World churches. The work of Wycliffe Bible Translators is a good example. Their help in translation efforts in the more than 4,000 languages still without a Bible is invaluable.

Three, there are short-term discipleship experiences that I think are especially valuable. Organizations like Operation Mobilization and W.E.C. have had a catalytic impact on both Asian and Western churches. These are discipleship-building ministries that benefit the Western participants as well as Asia's unevangelized millions.

Through cross-cultural and interracial contact, such ministries are especially helpful because they allow Westerners to get a better understanding of the situation in Asia. Alumni of these programs are helping others in the West understand the real needs of the Two-Thirds World.

And, of course, there is the simple fact that the Holy Spirit does call individuals from one culture to witness to another. When He calls, we should by all means respond.

QUESTION: Why don't indigenous churches support their own missionaries in the Two-Thirds World?

ANSWER: They do. In fact, I believe most Asian Christians give a far greater portion of their income to missions than do Westerners. Scores of times I have seen them give chicken eggs, rice, mangoes and tapioca roots because they frequently do not have cash. The truth is that most growing churches in Asia are made up of people from the poor masses, many of whom live on less than US$1 per day.

As God's Spirit continues to move, many new mission boards are being formed. Some of the largest missionary societies in the world are now located in Asia. But in light of the need, we literally need hundreds of thousands of additional workers, who will, in turn, require more outside support.

Regrettably, there are some indigenous churches that do not support national evangelists for the same reason some Western congregations do not give—lack of vision and sin in the lives of the pastors and congregations. But this is no excuse for Western Christians to sit back and lose the greatest opportunity they have ever had to help win a lost world to Jesus.

QUESTION: Is there a danger that national missionary sponsorships will have a reverse effect by causing national workers to depend on the West for support rather than turning to the local churches?

ANSWER: The truth is, of course, that it is not outside money that weakens a growing church, but outside control. Money from the West actually liberates the missionaries and makes it possible for them to follow the call of God.

After generations of domination by Western colonialists, most Asians are acutely conscious of the potential problem of foreign control through outside money. It is frequently brought up in discussions by indigenous missionary leaders, and most indigenous missionary boards have developed policies and practices to provide for accountability without foreign control.

At Gospel for Asia, we have taken several steps to make sure funds get to local workers in a responsible way without destroying valuable local autonomy.

First, our selection process favors men and women who begin with a right attitude—those who are dependent on God for their support rather than on man.

Second, there is no direct or indirect supervision of the work by Western supporters. The donor gives the Lord's money to support the work of national missions through Gospel for Asia, and we, in turn, send the money to indigenous leaders who oversee the financial affairs on each field. Therefore, the national missionary is twice-removed from the source of the funds. This procedure is being followed by several other organizations that support national workers, and it seems to work very well.

Finally, as soon as a new work is established, the national missionary is able to begin branching out to nearby unreached villages. The new congregations he establishes will eventually gain enough financial stability to fully support him while still giving sacrificially to support missions. Many times, however, a successful missionary will be almost crippled by his ministry's rapid growth. When a great move of the Holy Spirit occurs in a village, the successful missionary may find he has several trained and gifted co-workers as "Timothys" who are ready to establish sister congregations. The rapid growth almost always outstrips the original congregation's ability to support him and the additional workers. This is when outside help is vitally needed.

Eventually, I am sure the indigenous churches will be able to support most pioneer evangelism, but the job is too big now without Western aid.

The quickest way to help Asian churches become self-supporting, I believe, is to support a growing indigenous missionary movement. As churches are established, the blessings of the Gospel will abound, and the new Asian believers will be able to support greater outreach. Sponsorship monies are like investment capital in the work of God. The best thing we can do to help make the Asian Church independent now is to support as many national missionaries as possible.

QUESTION: It seems as if I am getting fund-raising appeals every day from good Christian organizations. How can I know who is genuine and really in the center of God's will?

ANSWER: Obviously, you cannot respond to all the appeals, so what criteria should you use to make your decision? We have put together a few guidelines for mission giving, which I believe may be helpful. These are not absolutes, and not everything on the list will apply to every situation. Be sensitive to the Holy Spirit as you read through these thoughts. The Lord will be faithful to guide you.

- Do those asking for money believe in the fundamental truths of God's Word, or are they theologically liberal? Any mission that seeks to carry out God's work must be totally committed to His Word. Is the group asking for money affiliated with liberal organizations that deny the truth of the Gospel, while keeping the name "Christian"? Do their members openly declare their beliefs? Too many today walk in a gray area, taking no stands and trying to offend as few as possible so they can get money from all, whether friends or enemies of the cross of Christ. The Word of God is being fulfilled in them: "...having a form of godliness but denying its power" (2 Timothy 3:5).

- Is the goal of their mission to win souls, or are they only social-gospel oriented? The liberal person believes man is basically good; therefore, all that is needed to solve his problems is to change his environment. However, the Bible says all—rich and poor—must repent and come to Christ or be lost. You must know which gospel is being preached by the mission group asking for your support.

- Is the mission organization financially accountable? Do they use the money for the purpose for which it was given? Are their finances audited by independent auditors according to accepted procedures? Do they send an audited financial statement to anyone requesting it?

- Do members of the mission group live by faith or man's wisdom? God never changes His plan: "The just shall live by faith" (Galatians 3:11). When a mission continually sends out crisis appeals for its maintenance rather than for outreach, something is wrong with it. They seem to say, "God made a commitment, but now He is in trouble, and we must help Him out of some tight spot." God makes no promises He cannot keep. If a mission group constantly begs and pleads for money, you need to ask if they are doing what God wants them to do. We believe we must wait upon God for His mind and do only what He leads us to do, instead of taking foolish steps of faith without His going before us. The end should never justify the means.

- Finally, a word of caution. Do not look for a reason for not giving to the work of God. These points are only considerations to help guide you. Be open to the Spirit's leading as you decide how to give. Remember, we must give all we can, keeping only enough to meet our needs so the Gospel can be preached because "... the night is coming when no one can work" (John 9:4). The problem for most is not that we give too much, but that we give too little.

QUESTION: How can I help support national missionaries?

ANSWER: To support national missionaries through Gospel for Asia, all you need to do is the following:

- Visit Gospel for Asia online at www.gfa.org. Or mail in the pre-addressed reply card included in this book.

- Send in your first pledge payment. Most of our friends help support the work of national missions for $30 a month or more.

- Each month, as you continue your support, we will send you a statement. The lower portion of the statement can be returned in the envelope provided to send in your next month's support.

- If you prefer, you can arrange to have your monthly pledged support charged to a credit card or automatically withdrawn from your bank account.

- For every $30 pledge to support the work of national missions, you will receive a copy of a missionary's photo and personal testimony. This is the missionary you have the privilege of linking your life with, especially through your prayers. As soon as you receive information about your missionary, pray for him and his family every day.

- Periodically you will receive an update full of praise reports and prayer requests from the specific region where your missionary is working.

Appendix Two
Contact Information

For more information contact the
organization nearest you.

AUSTRALIA: Gospel for Asia Australia Inc.
               PO Box 3587
               Toowoomba QLD 4350
               Freephone: 1300 889 339
               info@gospelforasia.org.au

CANADA: Gospel for Asia
               245 King Street E
               Stoney Creek, ON L8G 1L9
               Toll-free: 1-888-WIN-ASIA
               info@gfa.ca

FINLAND: Gospel for Asia Finland ry
               PL 63, FI-65101, Vaasa
               Phone: 050 036 9699
               infofi@gfa.org

KOREA: 아시아복음선교회 한국지부
               (Gospel for Asia Korea)
               Seok-Am Blg 5th floor
               6-9 Tereran-ro 25 gil
               Yeoksam-dong, Gangnam-gu
               Seoul 135-080
               Toll-free: (080) 801-0191
               infokorea@gfa.org.kr

(more on next page)

NEW ZEALAND:

Gospel for Asia
PO Box 302580
North Harbour
Auckland 0751
Toll-free: 0800-819-819
infonz@gfa.org

SOUTH AFRICA:

Gospel for Asia (SA)
P.O. Box 28880
Sunridge Park
Port Elizabeth 6008
Phone: 041 360-0198
infoza@gfa.org

UNITED KINGDOM:

GOSPEL FOR ASIA (U.K.)
PO Box 316
Manchester M22 2DJ
Phone: 0161 946 9484
infouk@gfa.org

UNITED STATES:

Gospel for Asia, Inc.
1116 St. Thomas Way
Wills Point, TX 75169
Toll-free: 1-800-WIN-ASIA
info@gfa.org

Revolution in World Missions
has been published in these languages:

Chinese	Korean
English	Polish
Finnish	Portuguese
French	Spanish
German	

NOTES

Chapter 4: I Walked in a Daze

1. Robert L. Heilbroner, *The Great Ascent: The Struggle for Economic Development in Our Time* (New York, NY: Harper & Row, 1963), pp. 33–36.

2. Economic Research Service, U.S.D.A., "Percent of Consumer Expenditures Spent on Food, Alcoholic Beverages, and Tobacco That Were Consumed at Home, by Selected Countries, 2014" (http://www.ers.usda.gov/data-products/food-expenditures.aspx) (accessed April 11, 2016).

Chapter 5: A Nation Asleep in Bondage

1. Wycliffe Bible Translators, Inc., "Why Bible Translation?" (https://www.wycliffe.org/about/why) (accessed April 11, 2016).

2. Rochunga Pudaite, *My Billion Bible Dream* (Nashville, TN: Thomas Nelson Publishers, 1982), p. 129.

3. Jason Mandryk, *Operation World*, 7th ed. (Colorado Springs, CO: Biblica, 2010), p. 869.

4. David B. Barrett and Todd M. Johnson, eds., *World Christian Trends, AD 30-AD 2200* (Pasadena, CA: William Carey Library, 2001), p. 45.

5. *Ibid.*, pp. 417–419.

6. *Ibid.*, p. 40.

7. *Ibid.*, p. 60.

Chapter 8: A New Day in Missions

1. Mandryk, *Operation World*, 7th ed., pp. 215–216.

Chapter 9: Is Missions an Option?

1. The World Bank, "2015 World Development Indicators: Size of the Economy" (http://wdi.worldbank.org/table/1.1) (accessed April 11, 2016).

2. Barrett and Johnson, *World Christian Trends, AD 30-AD 2200*, p. 655.

3. *Ibid.*, p. 40.

Chapter 10: God Is Withholding Judgment

1. C.S. Lewis, *The Problem of Pain* (London, U.K.: Fontana Publishers, 1957), pp. 106–107.

2. Janet Benge and Geoff Benge, *C.T. Studd: No Retreat* (Seattle, WA: Youth With A Mission Publishing, 2005), p. 40.

Chapter 11: Why Should I Make Waves?

1. Barrett and Johnson, *World Christian Trends, AD 30-AD 2200*, p. 429.

2. Watchman Nee, *Love Not the World* (Fort Washington, PA: CLC, 1968), pp. 23–24.

Chapter 12: Hope Has Many Names

1. International Labour Organization, "Child Labour in Asia and the Pacific," (http://www.ilo.org/asia/areas/child-labour/lang--en/index.htm) (accessed August 11, 2016).

2. Human Rights Watch, "The Small Hands of Slavery: Bonded Child Labor in India," (https://www.hrw.org/reports/1996/India3.htm) (accessed April 11, 2016).

Chapter 13: Enemies of the Cross

1. Barrett and Johnson, *World Christian Trends, AD 30-AD 2200*, p. 32.

Chapter 14: A Global Vision

1. Dennis E. Clark, *The Third World and Mission* (Waco, TX: Word Books, 1971), p. 70.

2. Roland Allen, *The Spontaneous Expansion of the Church* (Grand Rapids, MI: William B. Eerdmans, 1962), p. 19.

3. Barrett and Johnson, *World Christian Trends, AD 30-AD 2200*, p. 421.

Chapter 16: The Church's Primary Task

1. George Verwer, *No Turning Back* (Wheaton, IL: Tyndale House Publishers, 1983), pp. 89–90.

Gospel for Asia's School of Discipleship

Encounter God | Know Him More

Your life will never be the same.

You will:

Transform the lives of Asia's hurting and oppressed by serving at Gospel for Asia's U.S. home office.

Learn to embrace spiritual disciplines through prayer, solitude and devotions.

Grow spiritually through classes that emphasize real-life application of God's Word.

Live a simple lifestyle focused on knowing Christ and making Him known.

Can you die to yourself for one year?

Learn more and get your free information kit.
gfa.org/oneyear

School of Discipleship is open to dedicated Christian single adults ages 18-27

gfa.org/school • /gfaschool • disciple365.org • @gfaschool

"I have never seen deeper growth in my life than during my time here."—Jordan

Get involved with God's work in Asia.

Your life can expand the work of national missionaries when you serve behind the scenes.

Become a Gospel for Asia Volunteer
- Share the ministry with others through social media and blogs.
- Hand out free books to challenge and inspire friends and family.
- Represent GFA at local events. (We'll train and equip you!)

Serve in a College Internship
- Gain work experience and grow spiritually, too.
- Programs are available for a range of majors.
- Internships may qualify for college credit.

Join GFA's Home Team Staff
- Serve behind the scenes to send Christ's love across the globe.
- Be part of a community that pursues Christ passionately in prayer and worship.
- Servant-hearted people with a variety of skills—from network administration to building maintenance—are needed.

Learn more about how you can get involved at

gfa.org/involved

Support missionaries *eager to go*
to villages in Asia needing to
know *God's love.*

Make a choice today that will forever change the fate
of those who have yet to hear.

See missionaries you can partner with at

gfa.org/missionaries

or contact the Gospel for Asia organization
nearest you. (See Appendix 2.)